EATING YOUR WAY TO
LOW
CHOLESTEROL

How I Lowered My Cholesterol Without Drugs

225 recipes with Guidelines and Tips

Jeannie Serpa

1st WORLD
PUBLISHING

EATING YOUR WAY TO
LOW CHOLESTEROL

Jeannie Serpa

© Jeanne A. Serpa 2009

Published by 1stWorld Publishing
P.O. Box 2211 Fairfield, Iowa 52556
tel: 641-209-5000 • fax: 866-440-5234
web: www.1stworldpublishing.com

First Edition

LCCN: 2009936292
SoftCover ISBN: 978-1-4218-9117-0
HardCover ISBN: 978-1-4218-9116-3
eBook ISBN: 978-1-4218-9118-7

This book is intended as a source of information only and is not a substitute for medical advice. The author is not a medical professional, and readers should consult a medical professional before embarking on this program. All efforts of this book have been based on research and personal experience. The accuracy of its information is based on facts as of this printing. The author expressly disclaims any responsibility for any adverse or unforeseen effects arising from the use of, or application of the information contained herein.

Table of Contents

Acknowledgements

It is with gratitude and humility that I thank the following for their invaluable help in getting this book to press:

My daughters, Mary Jane Gray and Joanne Morrissey.

Members of the South County Writers Group (Enid Flaherty, Tracy Hart, Virginia Leaper, Camilla Lee, Michael Grossman, and Richard Parker).

Dr. Kimberly Beauchamp, Dr. Carla Cesario, Normand Leclair, Cindy Lewis, Martha Murphy, Dave and Holley Serpa, Jack Serpa.

Nina Benjamin of 1st World Publishing.

The many friends and family members who have patiently listened and advised me over the four years of this book's journey.

Thank you, one and all!

Dedication

This book is dedicated to the memory of my brother, Robert Carroll, who died of a heart attack on January 15, 2008.

and

To my daughter Mary Jane Gray, who not only spent endless hours typing and filing recipes, but also believed in me and constantly cheered me on.

Foreword by Carla Cesario, MD

It is always heartening to me, in an age where prescription drugs are often considered the panacea, when a patient takes her healing in her own hands. This book is a welcome contribution to all of us who are concerned about our own health. After years of nutritional research, it has become apparent that it is not always high cholesterol that is hereditary, but our eating habits. The author raises a sobering point in Chapter 6, *Children and Cholesterol*. The legacy that we are leaving our children by years of eating pre-packaged, processed, "fast" foods that are high in animal fats becomes heart disease by the time a child reaches the age of eight.

A December 2008 issue of *Time Magazine* on the State of American Health revealed that for the first time in American history, the current generation of children will not live as long as their parents. The reason? Because of the way they eat. But, do not despair. We can reverse this disease, and that is precisely what the author has proven.

This book represents one woman's success story in the battle against heart disease, the number one killer of Americans. Anyone who has high cholesterol is at risk for heart disease. Her recipes are delicious and their ingredients are accessible to anyone. She even includes a section on children's recipes. Her journey and practical approaches to lowering cholesterol will inspire you to do the same. Read on, and cook your way to low cholesterol!

Foreword by Cindy Lewis, MS, RD, LDN

Jeannie Serpa has hit the mark with *Eating Your Way To Low Cholesterol*. The personal triumph of lowering her cholesterol by choosing foods low in saturated fats and full of soluble fiber should be an inspiration to those willing to commit to this mouthwatering program.

I would recommend this book to all my nutrition clients with and without high cholesterol. The recipes are sound and her use of herbs, spices, and other seasonings take the "boring" out of healthy eating!

A Must Read

Unlike Glossaries that most of us tend to glance over, this is one that you should read carefully. There is much confusion for us lay persons regarding all the medical terms involved with cholesterol. Examine this list with its simple, clear, concise definitions and use it for a reference as you read along *and* cook along!

GLOSSARY of TERMS

Arteries: Blood vessels that carry blood from the heart to various parts of the body.

Atherosclerosis: A disease in which the walls of the arteries become thick and irregular due to a buildup of plaque. As plaque builds up, the arteries are narrowed and the flow of blood is reduced.

Cholesterol: A fat-like, waxy substance present in foods that comes from animal sources, such as meat, fish, poultry, egg yolks, and whole milk dairy products. Most vegetables, fruit, and foods from plant sources have no cholesterol.

Heart Attack: Damage to the heart muscle due to an insufficient supply of blood.

High Density Lipoprotein: HDL, the "good" cholesterol, transports cholesterol to the liver where it is removed from the bloodstream. *THE HIGHER YOUR HDL, THE BETTER.*

Low Density Lipoproteins: LDL, the "bad" cholesterol and the main carrier of harmful cholesterol. *The HIGHER YOUR LDL, the GREATER the RISK of CORONARY HEART DISEASE.*

Monounsaturated Fat: "Good" fat found in olive oil, canola oil, nuts, and peanuts. Peanuts are not nuts. They are legumes.

Omega-3 Fatty Acids: These "good" unsaturated fats are present in such fish as: salmon, mackerel, bluefish, sardines, and albacore tuna. They are also found in walnuts and flaxseed.

Plaque: A deposit of fatty material on the inner lining of arterial walls.

Polyunsaturated Fats: Oils of vegetables that are liquid at room temperature, such as safflower, sunflower, corn, and soybean. Moderate intake advised.

Saturated Fat: "Bad" fats that are solid at room temperature, found in foods of animal origin such as: meat, butter, cheese, whole milk, and ice cream. Also, coconut, coconut oil, palm oil, and fried foods (except those fried in olive or canola oil). *SATURATED FAT CAN INCREASE YOUR LDL and CLOG YOUR ARTERIES.*

Soluble Fiber: Fiber that helps lower cholesterol. Soluble fiber dissolves in liquid and cleans out your arteries. Good examples of foods high in soluble fiber are: oats, barley, beans, nuts, and most fruits and vegetables.

Statin Drugs: These slow the body's production of cholesterol and assist the liver in removing "bad" cholesterol (LDL) that already exists in the blood. See **Introduction** for more information.

Stroke: Loss of muscle function, speech, vision, sensation, or speech resulting from brain cell damage caused by insufficient supply of blood to part of the brain.

Trans Fatty Acids: Hidden killers! These fats are produced when hydrogen is mixed with vegetable oil, producing a solid fat. Trans fats are found in shortening, lard, stick margarine (not soft tub margarine), French fries, doughnuts, and bakery goods.

THESE FATS RAISE BLOOD CHOLESTEROL. They raise LDL and lower HDL. We want our HDL to be as high as possible.

Triglycerides: A type of fat found in the blood, triglycerides are used by the body as a form of energy. *HIGH BLOOD LEVELS of TRIGLYCERIDES ADD to the RISK of HEART ATTACK.*

Unsaturated Fats: Monounsaturated fats and polyunsaturated fats are both unsaturated. These fats do *not* increase LDL cholesterol. They are usually derived from plant sources. Olive oil, canola oil, nuts, and avocados are good examples of unsaturated fats.

Introduction

(Required Reading)

High fat, low fat, saturated, unsaturated, monounsaturated, polyunsaturated, good fat, bad fat, HDL, LDL! Had enough? How about triglycerides and the latest, trans fats? If you are trying to lower your cholesterol level and are confused, take heart. You are not alone. Thousands of us face this dilemma. I lowered my own extremely high blood cholesterol by 96 points in just six weeks without the aid of drugs. Another six weeks brought even more success and netted an additional 29 points for a total reduction of 125. Did I follow the diet recommended by the American Heart Association? NO! What did I do that was different?

Here is my story.

I was sitting across from my long-time trusted personal physician who had just announced that she was worried about me. My total blood cholesterol level was 314! With a family history of heart attacks, something had to be done and fast. I left the office, clutching a copy of the American Heart Association Diet, full of determination and vowing that I would beat this monster. Just three weeks earlier my sister had suffered two successive heart attacks; a younger brother had already survived seven. My mom wore a pacemaker. As a mother of nine and grandmother of eighteen, I had more than enough incentive and immediately started the recommended AHA diet.

After assiduously following this diet for six weeks, there was no change. Was this high level due more to family tendencies than to food? I did not want to resort to a drug. My doctor insisted. The statin drug Lipitor was prescribed. At the end of nine days on Lipitor, my legs ached unbearably. A phone call to my doctor brought the following advice: "Continue the drug. There is a strong possibility that your body will adjust." But *my* body seemed to be screaming "Get out of here, I don't want it!" After thanking my doctor, I put down the phone, flushed the remaining tablets down the toilet and embarked on some serious research.

I studied charts, digested statistics, memorized numbers, and did the math. I read nutritional labels on packages only to find innumerable inconsistencies. What was going on here? I felt entangled in a jungle of information. I talked to family and friends faced with the same problem. I interviewed anyone I could find with high cholesterol, taking endless notes. At times I felt like Don Quixote, chasing windmills, but I was on a mission here and there had to be an easier way. It was soon clear why so many people were opting for a drug rather than wading through this quagmire of information. Was there a simpler solution? The answer is YES!

Out of all this research has emerged a clear, simple program for winning the battle against high cholesterol. No charts, no tables, no statistics, and no confusion. I started developing recipes, testing and retesting. I wanted delicious meals and snacks that would lower cholesterol *and* be quick and easy to prepare. Once I started eating generous amounts of the foods that are known to lower cholesterol, my level began to drop. Meanwhile, my doctor still thinking I was taking Lipitor, had ordered another blood test. At the follow up appointment she congratulated me crediting, of course, Lipitor. Imagine her surprise when I revealed that I hadn't been taking it, that this was all due to my own diet. Her interest spurred me on and led to sharing this program with others.

Before beginning this diet plan, review it with your physician. In many cases high cholesterol is genetic and he or she may advise that a statin drug is called for. Ask whether or not my food plan along with a drug is advisable. Request a blood test at the end of six weeks so that both of you can chart your progress. I cannot even begin to describe the elation you will feel when that level starts to descend. If I can do this, you can do it. Let's get started!

Chapter 1

What to Eat; What Not to Eat
(Always with 8 to 10 glasses of water every day)

THE FIGHTER FOODS

These are the warriors in the battle against your disease. These foods contain no cholesterol or "bad" saturated fats and most importantly, they are known to actually REDUCE cholesterol.

- Oat Bran
- Beans
- Olive Oil
- Barley
- Cinnamon
- Canola oil
- Rice bran
- Oatmeal
- Avocados

THE SAFE FOODS

You have innumerable choices. Here is a partial list. These have no cholesterol and little or no saturated fat and are a vital part of the program.

- Vegetables
- Fruits
- Herbs
- Rice

- Garlic
- Pasta
- Skim Milk
- Grains
- Non fat evaporated milk
- Plain fat free yogurt
- Fat free- 0 cholesterol Cool Whip*
- Fat free sour cream
- Egg whites and egg substitutes
- Soft tub margarine
- Fat free, no cholesterol products

* A WORD ABOUT COOL WHIP

Read the nutrition label on a container of Cool Whip and you will see that a single serving (2 tablespoons) has 0 cholesterol, 0 saturated fat and 0 trans fat. Sounds good, right? Read the ingredients, however, and you will see that hydrogenated vegetable oil is listed. While hydrogenated vegetable oil is not as bad for us as partially hydrogenated vegetable oil, we should still use Cool Whip in moderation. In 2006 the FDA ruled that as long as a single serving of trans fat or partially hydrogenated vegetable oil did not exceed 0.5 grams, it did not have to be listed on the nutrition label. With this in mind, if you were to consume 4 servings, that would add up to 1.6 grams trans fat. The package claims the product contains 0 grams of trans fat. Remember this is only if you consume only one serving size. I have used Cool Whip in a number of recipes, staying well within the recommended amounts. Nevertheless, I urge you not to overdo its use. Make these recipes as special treats and always consult your doctor for advice.

SAFE SNACKS, SWEETS and CONDIMENTS

Food should be a pleasure. This is not about sacrifice and deprivation. Use the following "treats" as rewards.

- Hard candy*
- Gum drops, or spice drops*
- Jelly beans*
- *Baked* potato chips
- *Baked* pretzels
- Sherbet
- Natural popcorn (butter free or 94% fat free)
- Fat free frozen yogurt (Kemp's is very close in taste to ice cream)
- Fat free sorbet
- Gelato
- Jell-O
- Pickles, relish, catsup
- Cranberry sauce
- Honey, mustard, salsa, chutney

* *High in sugar; don't overdo*

LOW FAT, LOW CHOLESTEROL WINNERS

Our bodies do need some fat and some cholesterol. It is also extremely important that we ingest adequate amounts of protein every day. All of the following are high in protein and low in saturated "bad" fat. The fish and shellfish are high in omega-3. Recommended serving size for the following is 4-6 ounces.

- Turkey with skin removed
- Chicken with skin removed
- Fish
- Wild game, such as buffalo, elk, venison, kangaroo
- Clams, oysters, scallops, snails
- Lobster, crab, crayfish, squid
- Rice and beans in combination (These combine to produce a perfect protein.)
- Lean beef, veal, lamb with all fat trimmed. Have *occasionally.**
- Pork, the lean, more expensive cuts with all fat trimmed. Have *occasionally**

* *Beef, veal, lamb, and pork should be introduced only after your cholesterol has been reduced to the number recommended for you by your physician.*

If you are concerned about lean meats tasting dry, marinate in olive or canola oil for 20 minutes or more. For tougher cuts of meat, add a little vinegar or lemon juice to the oil and marinate for up to two hours. Always refrigerate in the marinade and pour off and discard it before cooking.

THE NUTTY TRUTH

Nuts, nut butters, peanuts, and peanut butter deserve a special listing. All are high in fats. These fats, for the most part, are "good fats" but they also contain some saturated fat. Peanuts are a legume and not a nut but they fall into the same category when it comes to cholesterol. A study published in March 1993 by the New England Journal of Medicine found concrete evidence that nuts, in spite of their high fat content, have a lowering effect on cholesterol.

THE MOST HARMFUL FOODS

For the time being, look upon these foods as poison. Just for now, envision them with skull and crossbones. Do not let this discourage you! If you faithfully adhere to my diet plan, in a short time you may be able to add them in small amounts and in moderation.

- Butter
- Stick margarine
- Meats, such as beef, lamb, pork, and veal that are untrimmed of fat
- Duck
- Goose
- Chicken and turkey *with skin*
- Bacon (opt for the leaner Canadian bacon)
- Egg yolks *
- Whole milk, cream, yogurt, sour cream, any full fat dairy products
- Coconut (looks so harmless, but high in saturated fat)
- Any food cooked in fats other than canola or olive oil

- Deli lunch meats: except for those with no saturated fat
- Snacks: such as potato chips deep fried in saturated fat.
- Partially hydrogenated vegetable oils
- Any foods containing trans fat

* One extra large egg yolk can have up to 250 grams of cholesterol. The American Medical Association recommends no more than 300 grams per day in order to lower total cholesterol. 300 grams is often too generous. When I first started this plan I found 250 grams was far better. At this rate, a single extra large egg would equal an entire day's full quota. Need I say more? Incidentally, I no longer add up grams, nor should you. Just by following the guidelines in this program my former total cholesterol of 314 is holding strong at 189.

Recent studies suggest that eating 4 or 5 eggs a week is not harmful. These studies, as of this writing, are being questioned. The problem with many food studies is that they are often financed (or even conducted) by the very industry that produces the food itself.

Chapter 2

The Scoop on Oat Bran, Oatmeal, and Cold Oat Cereals

You have, no doubt, noted that oat bran is at the very top of my list of **FIGHTER FOODS**. Dr. James W. Anderson at the University of Kentucky is a pioneer researcher whose studies on oat bran and its value in the battle against high cholesterol have been an inspiration to me in developing my diet. Also on the list of **FIGHTER FOODS** is oatmeal. Is there a difference? Most decidedly, yes! Simply put, the difference is that oat bran has more soluble fiber than oatmeal. It is a proven fact that soluble fiber lowers blood cholesterol. (See definition of soluble fiber listed in the GLOSSARY of TERMS.)

When we scan the nutrition labels on some products, we will see Dietary Fiber as well as Soluble Fiber. We need both. However, it is important to note the difference between the two. To compound the confusion, some labels list Total Fiber. The inconsistencies in labeling can be frustrating, but for our purposes we need to zero in on Soluble Fiber. Just seven grams a day have been enough to dramatically lower my own cholesterol.

SHOPPING for OAT BRAN

When shopping for oat bran, keep in mind that what we are talking about here is oat bran hot cereal, available in most supermarkets. If oat bran is a new product to you, the first time shopping for it can be confusing. Many people have told me they have difficulty locating it on the shelves. Look in the Hot Cereal Section for a box that measures about 4 ½ x 7 ½ inches. There are many oat *meal* (not bran) cereals with the same size box that offer individual serving size packets of sweetened flavored oatmeal. Stay away from these. You want the real thing, pure and simple. The box you are looking for will be clearly labeled "Oat Bran Hot Cereal."

You may wish to eat it as a hot cereal as well as use it in the many recipes in this book. I started developing cookies made with oat bran and went on to cupcakes, quick breads, and muffins. Dr. Anderson's findings alone would have kept me baking, testing, and tasting, but it was the response from family and friends that cheered me on.

SO WHAT ABOUT OATMEAL and COLD OAT CEREALS?

Oatmeal is right up there with oat bran on my list of FIGHTER FOODS. The difference between the two is that oat bran has three grams of soluble fiber per serving, while oat meal has 2 grams per serving. As to the cold cereal Cheerios, it has only 1 gram. Cheerios is a fine nutritious cereal but it would take 3 cupfuls of it to attain the 3 grams found in oat bran. Vary your choices and enjoy all three.

Chapter 3

Beans, Oils, and Cinnamon

ABOUT BEANS

Black beans, red beans, white beans, kidney, broad beans, cranberry, scarlet runner, pinto, cow peas, black eyed peas, adzuki. There are so many varieties to choose from and endless ways to prepare them. While we may remember the good old fashioned baked-from-scratch beans that Grandma used to make, her version very probably contained large amounts of salt pork or bacon, both loaded with saturated fat. In the recipe section of this book you'll find much safer alternatives with no sacrifice in flavor.

With the huge variety of beans available in the form of soups, dips, salads, hummus, and casseroles (many being sold in ready-to-eat form), you may find yourself happily eating more than you ever did in your life. If gas is a problem, use Beano, a tablet available in supermarkets and pharmacies. If you are baking dried beans, when soaking them always drain off the water and add fresh water to the recipe. Dr. Michelle Moore suggests stirring a teaspoon of baking soda into the beans before baking.

TIME FOR AN OIL CHANGE?

Oils and fats require a little discussion. Olive oil and canola are known to lower cholesterol, so use these for cooking, baking and in salads. Do not use other oils, butter, stick margarine, lard, or shortening.*

> ** Store bought, bakery and restaurant baked goods are usually made with lard or shortening. Webster's dictionary defines lard as "A solid or semi-solid fat obtained by rendering pork fat." The Reader's Digest Oxford Word Finder defines it as " The internal fat of the abdomen of pigs, especially when rendered and clarified for use in cooking." This is saturated fat. Saturated fat clogs arteries. Is this what you want to put into your body?*

*There are a dozen recipes for truly delicious muffins in this book, plus a number of additional baked goods. All are made with canola oil, a fat that has been proven to **reduce** cholesterol. In addition, all contain oat bran. Oat bran has 3 grams of soluble fiber in each ½ cup. **Soluble fiber keeps our arteries clean!***

> **WARNING:** *Watch out for cake mixes and canned ready-to-use frostings. Read ingredients carefully. Cake mixes contain shortening and partially hydrogenated vegetable oil (trans fat). Although the nutrition label may read 0 trans fat, remember that is for a single serving, which is only 1/12 of a cake, quite a small slice!*

Ingredients on a typical can of frosting are shocking: animal shortening, beef fat, and lard! Play it safe. Make your own frosting. See my recipe for Low Cholesterol Chocolate Icing that accompanies "LET THEM EAT CAKE" CAKE.

Make use of the good oils listed under **FIGHTER FOODS** in Chapter 1. Before cooking, add a teaspoon of canola oil plus a pinch of thyme to fresh or frozen peas, green beans, or broccoli. Try olive oil with a sprinkle of herb/garlic seasoning added to spinach, kale, or tomatoes.

Skip the butter on baked potatoes. Add canola oil or a mild olive oil with a generous squeeze of lemon juice and celery salt instead. This helps to reduce cholesterol while providing flavor and that's what it's all about. Am I suggesting that you start pouring these good oils on every possible dish? *Certainly not!* Moderation is the key to good health. Just be sure to use them as substitutes for butter, stick margarine, or any oil that is high in saturated fat.

SOFT TUB MARGARINE vs. STICK MARGARINE vs. BUTTER

Why do I place soft tub margarine on the **SAFE FOODS** list in Chapter 1, yet list stick margarine under **THE MOST HARMFUL FOODS?** Stick margarine is high in saturated fat, trans fat, and cholesterol, while its soft cousin contains 0 cholesterol, 0 trans fat and is fairly low in saturated fat. Butter, of course, is the worst culprit of all. Yes, I know. I love, love, love it too! But take heart. Once you have your cholesterol level down to where your doctor says it should be, here's another tip that comes from Dr. Moore: Combine equal parts of butter and canola oil. Blend in your food processor until smooth and enjoy *in moderation*.

SALAD DRESSINGS

Although I've spent seemingly endless hours studying nutrition labels and scanning ingredient listings in order to save my readers this chore, there are times when you must check for yourself. This is especially true when it comes to store bought salad dressings. Look for 0 saturated fat, 0 cholesterol and 0 trans fat. Be especially careful of any listing that reads "partially hydrogenated vegetable oil." THIS IS TRANS FAT!

There are a host of safe and savory dressings on the market, but it pays to do your homework. A basic dressing of extra virgin olive oil with vinegar or lemon juice, jazzed up with herbs, whether commercially bottled or homemade, far exceeds the heavier fat and high cholesterol varieties. If you simply must have a topping for your greens that is both creamy and zesty, you'll love this: Mix a heaping teaspoon of ketchup or chili sauce into a six ounce container of fat free plain yogurt. Pep it up with a few drops of hot pepper sauce.

WELCOME, CINNAMON!

As of this writing, this important spice is the newest kid on the block, well deserving of a position on my list of **FIGHTER FOODS**. I applaud researchers Richard Anderson at the U.S. Department of Agriculture's Human Nutrition Center in Beltsville, Maryland, and Alam Khan of the NWFP Agriculture University in Pakistan for their findings on cinnamon as a cholesterol reducer. I had been using cinnamon in many of the recipes for this program simply for its marvelous flavor. Overjoyed with this news, I immediately increased the quantity in each and every recipe. I'm also adding it to decaf coffee grounds before brewing and adding a generous sprinkle to fat free plain yogurt. *As little as ½ teaspoon a day is effective and even a stick of cinnamon in a cup of tea helps.*

An interesting note here is that Anderson and Khan were actually researching cinnamon in respect to treating Type 2 diabetes. They discovered by accident that it not only helped those who have Type 2 diabetes, but those with cholesterol issues as well.

Chapter 4

Exercise? Oh Dear!

Let's face it. Everyone needs to exercise in order to stay fit. However, exercise is especially good for those of you with high cholesterol. Your arteries have narrowed from a build up of cholesterol and fat. Exercise helps the blood to flow through these vessels more easily. In addition to aiding blood flow, you get to enjoy a number of fringe benefits. You will be helping to:

1. keep your weight down
2. handle stress better
3. feel more relaxed
4. feel better about your appearance
5. increase energy and endurance
6. build stronger muscles

Having said all this, I must confess that when I started this program, I was a non-exerciser. Not only was I not an exercise buff, I was really quite sedentary, with no particular passion for fitness. Those of you out there who already golf, swim, play tennis, or engage in some type of regular physical activity have the added advantage of not having to suddenly introduce exercise into your lifestyle. Although I had been maintaining a cholesterol level of 189 (a total drop of 125 points) for four months, I knew in my heart of hearts that a bit of moving about would certainly add to my general state of fitness. I cannot stress enough the importance of checking with your doctor before embarking on any exercise regime. Mine has been quite moderate: simply walking 30-45 minutes a day three or four days a week and lifting three pound weights on opposite days.

At this point you may be thinking that this is just too much trouble. Consider carefully the risks you may be taking otherwise:

1. Heart attack   *2. Stroke*

3. Atherosclerosis   *4. Stress for your family*

5. Medical costs   *6. Time lost from work*

7. Possible surgery   *8. A shorter life*

Am I frightening you? I certainly hope so!

On a more positive note, exercise is closely linked to higher HDL levels. Keep in mind that HDL is the good cholesterol. Remember, "H is for High and Happy." Higher levels of HDL are known to lower the risk of coronary artery disease.

GETTING STARTED

If physical activity hasn't been a regular part of your day, you'll want to start slowly. Always talk with your doctor before starting any exercise plan. Every case is different and there are many factors to consider such as blood pressure, heart condition, muscle or joint problems, and diabetes to mention a few.

For me and for many others, getting "psyched up" and motivated is half the battle. It is important that we enjoy our chosen activity. We need to dance, play, have FUN! For some, an exercise class may be the answer. If you haven't been particularly active, it can be difficult to get started on a regular exercise routine. Common excuses are:

1. *I don't have time*   2. *I'm not a gym person*

3. *I'm out of shape*   4. *I'm too old*

5. *I'm too tired to exercise*   6. *It hurts*

7. *I don't like to sweat*   8. *I hate exercise*

Let us address each one of these excuses:

1. I don't have time.

We have all been given 24 hours a day. Most of us make time for things that we believe are important. How much do we value our health? Simply walking 20 to 30 minutes a day 4 days a week can make a sizable difference.

2. I'm not a gym person.

Do you dislike the gym atmosphere? Do you prefer a more private setting? You need not join a fitness club or go to a class. Try working out in your home while watching TV, listening to music, talking on the phone. Walk in your neighborhood or several times around a parking lot, climb stairs, dance in your kitchen, skip (when no one is looking). Whatever it takes to get you moving.

3. I'm out of shape.

Start slowly, perhaps with a five minute walk before breakfast or on a coffee or lunch break. Use the stairs instead of the elevator for one flight, gradually increasing a flight each week. The important thing here is try to do some little thing but do it gradually and faithfully. You will be amazed at how quickly your endurance will increase. Slow but steady wins the race and remember: Exercise does not have to be strenuous to be beneficial.

4. I'm too old.

No excuse at all. No, no, no! "The older the fiddler, the better the tune." Older people are often retired, have more time, and, especially if living alone, derive an added benefit from the social side of group exercise, whether a walking club or other group activity. No matter what your age, it is never too late to start. Healthy aging starts with physical activity.

5. I'm too tired.

Contrary to common belief, exercise actually counters feelings of fatigue. Regular exercise rewards us with increased energy and helps us sleep better too.

6. It hurts!

Exercise should not be painful. First and foremost let's dispel that myth, "no pain, no gain." If your chosen form of exercise is causing you discomfort, consider the following:

—Are you doing the wrong type of exercise for you?

—Have you started out too fast or too hard?

—Are you engaging in an exercise that could be aggravating an old injury?

—Is your activity too weight bearing or too high impact for your body?*

* Examples of High Impact activity are:

- *Jogging*
- *Aerobic dancing*
- *Basketball*
- *Racquet ball*
- *Rope skipping*
- *Tennis*

*Examples of Low Impact activity are:

- *Walking*
- *Stair climbing*
- *Swimming*
- *Water aerobics*
- *Bicycling*
- *Slow dancing*

There is a major difference between injurious pain and the common muscle soreness that we should expect at the beginning of a new exercise. Learn to recognize the difference and consult your doctor for guidance.

7. I don't like to sweat.

Neither do I! My mother used to say that horses sweat, men perspire, but women glow. I'm all for glowing, yet I do recognize that most exercise books and magazine articles emphasize the value of working up a good sweat. This certainly has its merits but we can't always shower, especially after exercising on a lunch break. Since we've already established that even mild activity is beneficial, suffice it to say that those of us who wish only to glow are still reaping rewards. For those of you out there who are comfortable with more strenuous activity, go for it! If you are returning to a vigorous exercise program after having abandoned it for whatever reason (illness, injury, surgery, or just plain neglect) start slowly and gradually work up to your former level. You will be less apt to suffer unnecessary pain and injury. It is important to remember that you do not have to be an athlete to regain fitness nor is it necessary to play a strenuous game of tennis or run a marathon. Just get moving!

8. I hate to exercise.

So do I and so do millions of others. Get over it!

Chapter 5

What About Weight?

Since exercise and weight seem to work in tandem, weight issues are the next logical concern. Are you likely to lose weight if you follow my suggested food plan? Could you gain?

Here is a report on my own personal experience:

LOSING the FIRST TWO POUNDS

Those first six weeks of following my low/no cholesterol diet resulted in the loss of two pounds. Mind you, I was not thinking of weight at this point. I was concentrating only on lowering that too high level of 314. The loss of two pounds came as a pleasant surprise, and this was before adding exercise to the program!

GAINING IT BACK and WHY

By the end of the second six week period my level had dropped to 238, however the two pounds were back, accompanied by two more! It didn't take long to figure out why. I had been at work developing new recipes: experimenting and *tasting*, changing ingredients and *tasting*, cooking, baking and *tasting*. Meanwhile, my caloric intake (unbeknownst to me) had been steadily increasing and, although the basic *foods* hadn't changed the *amounts* had! In one day I might be testing five different muffin recipes, consuming five muffins instead of the recommended three. Perhaps those baked beans were not tasty enough so it was necessary to adjust the ingredients, whip up another batch and test those. Such fun! Reasons for the weight gain were evident, however additional recipes were needed in order to complete a diet that was deliciously appealing and would successfully lower cholesterol. I was fully committed to continue inventing more recipes, but it was imperative that I keep the tasting and testing under control.

CONCLUSION:

Like any food plan, this one will not cause weight gain unless you abuse it and you could lose weight as I did before I started all that tasting and testing!

Chapter 6

Children and Cholesterol

Many of us regard high cholesterol and heart disease as problems belonging to adults, particularly older adults. However, we are hearing more and more about forty and fifty year olds dying of heart attacks. Consider the number of teenagers who have, without any prior symptoms, died on playing fields or at sports practice. Autopsies have revealed that these young, seemingly healthy children had clogged arteries. Unfortunately, this insidious disease shows no outward signs, thus indicating a need for early testing for children whose families have histories of heart disease.

High levels of cholesterol are a major factor contributing to heart attacks and stroke. Medical research reveals that that cardiovascular disease begins in childhood. It's important to know your child's cholesterol levels, especially if there's a family history of heart disease.

Just how at risk are our children and grandchildren? Should we be concerned? And, if so, what can we do to protect them?

Much can and is being done. Pediatricians and cardiologists are becoming more and more aware of the problem and are beginning to take proper precautions. Testing for cholesterol in children has been somewhat controversial, yet some doctors advise testing for elevated cholesterol levels in toddlers as young as two *when there are genetic concerns*. Others say that all adults, even those with no genetic concerns should be tested by the time they are twenty years old. Parents, however, often need to take the initiative themselves and demand proper testing for young children, even babies, when there is cause for concern.

In January 2007 I did an informal mini survey in my own family to find out if pediatricians were addressing the problem. None of my eighteen grandchildren had been tested for high levels of cholesterol, in spite of the fact that heart disease runs rampant in both sides of their families. However, in all instances, doctors did a thorough job of checking on diet, exercise, and weight, and teenagers were asked about smoking. Their parents felt secure and were confident that these excellent doctors would order blood tests if warranted.

Flash forward to July 2009. Good news! Two of my granddaughters (age 17 and 18) were asked by their doctors about any history of heart disease or high levels of cholesterol in their families. When they relayed the information about our family, both doctors immediately ordered blood tests for both girls and both, thankfully, had acceptable levels.

In a study conducted by Dr. Henry McGill of the Southwest Foundation for Biomedical Research in San Antonio, Texas, autopsies of 760 young men and women who had died from accidents or homicides revealed that all had clogged arteries. One in 500 children are born with a condition known as familial hypercholesterolemia (genetically elevated cholesterol levels). Their arteries clog while they are very young and, if not treated, they die of heart attacks in their teens or early twenties.

For most children with higher than normal levels the solution is a matter of adjusting lifestyle. The same recipes for adults offered in this book can be applied to children's diets. Most kids like to cook and are more likely to eat foods that they invent or prepare themselves.

I recently checked bookstores and the library for children's cookbooks. Every single one of them were for youngsters who were old enough to use the stove and oven. Nothing out there for the four to eight year olds, so I decided to include some recipes that my own small grandchildren make with me. See Children's Recipes.

Appetizers & Dips

CHIVE DIP

While most dips are high in saturated fat and cholesterol, the use of fat free sour cream and yogurt makes this a worry free treat for us cholesterol fighters.

Ingredients

1 ½ cups fat free sour cream

½ cup fat free plain yogurt

½ cup minced chives

½ teaspoon coarse ground black pepper

½ teaspoon sea salt

¼ - ½ teaspoon hot sauce, according to taste

Procedure

Thoroughly combine all ingredients. Transfer to a bowl and chill for at least 30 minutes before serving, allowing flavors to meld. Place in the center of a pretty platter surrounded by crudités (raw vegetables) and/or rice crackers.

Yield: 2 cups.

CILANTRO HUMMUS with WALNUTS

This is a different spin on the traditional pesto, which is made with basil and pine nuts. The cilantro gives this version a little "bite" with a refreshing flavor. Both Garbanzo beans and walnuts are high on the list of cholesterol reducing foods.

cont...

47

Ingredients

15 ounce can garbanzo beans (drain and reserve liquid)
3 tablespoons reserved garbanzo liquid
½ cup walnuts
3 tablespoons extra virgin olive oil
3 tablespoons fresh lemon juice
⅔ cup cilantro leaves (do not pack down)
1 clove garlic, peeled
⅛ teaspoon coarse ground black pepper
¼ teaspoon sea salt

Procedure

Place all ingredients in a blender and process until smooth. Serve as a dip with crackers or as a delicious sauce for pasta.

CRAB SALAD STUFFED TOMATOES
in LETTUCE CUPS

The perfect pretty salad for a ladies' summer luncheon. Present with a side of green beans or asparagus and warm rolls. Iced tea and sorbet round out the meal nicely and it's all cholesterol safe!

Ingredients

½ cup slivered almonds
1 head iceberg lettuce
4 large red ripe tomatoes
3 tablespoons reduced fat mayonnaise
1 tablespoon fresh lemon juice

cont...

1 tablespoon canola oil

1 tablespoon minced chives or sweet onion

1 large stalk celery, peeled and chopped small

1 tablespoon grated carrots

½ teaspoon dried dill weed

1 teaspoon chopped fresh parsley

14 ounces cooked crabmeat or imitation crabmeat, chopped

Sea salt to taste

Fresh ground black pepper to taste

Smoked sweet paprika

Procedure

Place the almonds in a dry skillet and toast over medium heat until golden and fragrant, about 5-10 minutes. Remove from pan and set aside to cool.

Remove core from lettuce, keeping the head intact. Remove any unattractive outer leaves. Clean by holding under cold running water; shake out excess water. Carefully separate the leafy cups and place upside down on paper towels to drain.

Slice the top third from each tomato. Scoop out the insides, being careful to keep the tomato "shell" intact. Discard the insides or save for another use. For a decorative touch, use a sharp knife to cut little V's along the top edge.

Thoroughly combine mayonnaise, lemon juice, canola oil, chives, celery, carrots, dill, and parsley. Gently fold in the crabmeat. Add salt and pepper to taste. Fill the tomato shells with the crabmeat salad and sprinkle very lightly with paprika. When ready to serve place a lettuce shell on each of 4 salad plates and then a stuffed tomato inside each cup. Scatter the toasted almonds on top.

Serves 4.

DIP with ZIP

Here's a dip with lots of flavor and a bit of a bite. Serving baked pota-to chips and rice crackers with this assures us of an appetizer that is free of trans fat, saturated fat, and cholesterol. Colorful crudités such as carrot strips, celery, grape tomatoes, and broccoli florets provide plenty of soluble fiber. Remember, soluble fiber removes plaque from our arteries!

Ingredients

1 cup Yogurt Cheese*

¼ teaspoon dried basil or ¾ teaspoon finely chopped fresh

¼ teaspoon paprika

1 teaspoon dried onion flakes or 2 teaspoons fresh minced
   Vidalia onion

½ teaspoon sugar

½ teaspoon prepared horseradish

Pinch of garlic powder

Procedure

Combine all ingredients in a small bowl. Refrigerate and allow flavors to marry. Transfer to a dip dish, center on a platter and surround with baked potato chips and rice crackers.

Yields 1 cup.

*YOGURT CHEESE

Place 12 ounces of plain fat free yogurt in a strainer that has been lined with a large disposable coffee filter. Place in refrigerator and allow to drain for a few hours or overnight. Discard liquid. Yogurt cheese can be used plain (it's delicious; I like it better than full fat cream cheese) or as a base for dips and spreads.

Yield: 1 cup.

DIPPITY DILL DIP with CRUDITES

An all around healthy, crunchy, and delicious appetizer. Besides being protein rich and free of those of harmful fats that cholesterol watchers must avoid, my Dippity Dill Dip is full of zippy flavor. The colorful array of vegetables provide soluble fiber, vitamins, and antioxidants. Altogether an impressive presentation.

Ingredients

1 cup fat free Yogurt Cheese (see page 50)

1 tablespoon minced fresh or 1 teaspoon dried dill

1 tablespoon minced sweet onion or 1 teaspoon dried onion flakes

Dash of hot pepper sauce

Peeled raw carrot sticks (or store bought peeled baby carrots)

Celery sticks, well peeled to avoid strings

Baby broccoli florets, fresh (or frozen and thawed)

Baby cauliflower florets, fresh (or frozen and thawed)

Cherry or grape tomatoes

Paprika and chopped parsley for garnish

Procedure

Mix together the Yogurt Cheese, dill, onion, and pepper sauce. Refrigerate for 20-30 minutes to allow flavors to blend. Meanwhile, wash and prepare carrots, celery, broccoli, cauliflower, and tomatoes. Place dip mixture in a small bowl or dip dish and center it on a platter. Sprinkle with paprika and parsley. Surround the dip with nicely arranged vegetables. For a large crowd, increase ingredients accordingly.

HERB CHEESE SPREAD in a BREAD BOWL

An extraordinarily delicious appetizer that makes an impressive presentation. Check ingredients label on the bread before buying or ask your baker to be sure that neither shortening nor lard has been used in the bread. Both are made from refined pig fat. (See Webster's dictionary.) There are plenty of good breads out there that are free of these dangerous ingredients.

Ingredients

1 cup Yogurt Cheese (see page 50)

1 tablespoon chopped fresh thyme or 1 teaspoon dried

1 tablespoon chopped fresh marjoram or 1 teaspoon dried

1 tablespoon minced parsley

½ teaspoon freshly ground black pepper

1 teaspoon fresh lemon juice

½ cup fat free sour cream

1 round loaf crusty bread

Procedure

With a fork, whip together Yogurt Cheese with thyme, marjoram, parsley, pepper, and lemon juice until light and fluffy. Stir in the sour cream. Chill one hour before serving, allowing the flavors to marry. When ready to serve, make a bread bowl by cutting out the inside of the bread in large chunks. Fill the center with Herb Cheese, place on a serving platter and surround with the chunks of bread.

Makes 1 ½ cups.

HERB DIP

Vegetables are a fine source of soluble fiber. Soluble fiber helps us to outsmart high cholesterol. Serve this tasty herb dish with crudités, and help clean out those arteries.

Ingredients

⅔ cup reduced fat or fat free mayonnaise

1 cup fat free sour cream

1 tablespoon minced onion

1 tablespoon parsley

1 teaspoon dill weed

1 ½ teaspoons Beau Monde seasoning

1 tablespoon lemon juice

Dash of salt

Procedure

Combine all ingredients and chill. Serve with crudités (an assortment of raw vegetables such as carrot sticks, celery, cherry tomatoes, and broccoli florets).

HOT CRAB DIP

Savor the crab flavor but indulge with care. There are low amounts of saturated fat and cholesterol in this dip, so enjoy only if your doctor is satisfied with your cholesterol count.

Preheat oven to 350°

Ingredients

6 ounces cooked crab meat or imitation crab
¼ cup reduced fat mayonnaise
8 ounces reduced fat cream cheese
2 tablespoons milk
1 tablespoon minced fresh parsley or 1 teaspoon dried
1 tablespoon minced chives
1 tablespoon fresh lemon juice
½ teaspoon onion powder
½ to 1 teaspoon prepared horseradish, according to taste
Sea salt
Coarse ground black pepper

Procedure

Break up crab meat or chop imitation crab and combine with mayonnaise. Combine cheese with milk and add to crab mixture, then add parsley, chives, lemon juice, onion powder, and horseradish. Season to taste with salt and pepper. Transfer to a baking dish and heat for 20 to 25 minutes or until bubbly and lightly brown on the edges. Serve warm with rice crackers and baked potato chips.

Makes about 2 cups.

LOBSTER SALAD MINI TARTS

These make a perfectly delectable and cholesterol friendly appetizer. You may wish to substitute cooked crabmeat or imitation crab for the lobster. Double or triple the recipe for a large crowd. For added crispness, arrange frozen tarts on a cookie sheet ahead of time and bake in a 350° oven for 5 minutes or until golden brown. Allow tarts to cool before filling.

Ingredients

¾ pound cooked lobster meat

½ teaspoon dried dill

1 tablespoon finely chopped celery

⅛ teaspoon dried tarragon

4 tablespoons mock crème fraîche*

3 tablespoons reduced or fat free mayonnaise

1 teaspoon fresh lemon juice

Sea salt and white pepper to taste

2 packages frozen mini tarts (Athens is an excellent brand with 0 saturated fat and 0 trans fat)

Procedure

Drain any liquid from the lobster and chop fine. Place in a medium size bowl and add dill, celery, tarragon, mock crème fraîche, mayonnaise, lemon juice, salt, and pepper. Combine thoroughly. Fill each tart with the lobster salad and arrange on an attractive platter.

Makes 24 -30 pieces.

*To make the mock crème fraîche

Combine 2 tablespoons fat free sour cream and 2 tablespoons fat free Cool Whip.

MAKE YOUR OWN POTATO CHIPS

Preheat oven to 425°

Ingredients

3 large red skin potatoes (substitute Idaho or Russet)
Extra virgin olive oil
Coarse sea salt
Fresh ground black pepper
Sweet paprika

Procedure

Scrub red potatoes, leave skins intact and slice about ⅛ inch thick. If you are using Idaho or Russet potatoes you may wish to peel them. Layer the slices on a non stick cookie sheet and brush each slice with olive oil. Sprinkle with salt, pepper, and paprika. For garlicky chips, substitute garlic salt for the sea salt. Bake 10 to 15 minutes or until golden brown and crisp. Place on paper towels; adjust seasonings and transfer to a serving dish.

Variation

Substitute sweet potatoes or yams.

MARINATED MUSHROOMS

Serve these as an hors d'oeuvre with plenty of cocktail picks. I guarantee they will not last long! Use also as a salad topping or an accompaniment to poultry or fish. The recipe may be doubled and quart size jars can be used. Be sure to cool completely before covering and placing in the refrigerator.

cont...

Ingredients

1 pound white button mushrooms

2 cups cold water

1 teaspoon sea salt

½ cup extra virgin olive oil

¾ cup red wine vinegar

1 teaspoon sea salt

2 teaspoons granulated sugar

2 tablespoons finely chopped fresh tarragon leaves or ¾ teaspoon dried

2 tablespoons fresh rosemary needles or ¾ teaspoon dried

6-8 pearl or cippoline onions, peeled and halved

2 cloves garlic, peeled and halved

1 tablespoon coarse black pepper

1 teaspoon allspice

Procedure

Wipe mushrooms with a damp dish towel. Do not wash directly in water as this will toughen them. Remove stems. Make a small slit in each mushroom cap, being sure not to cut all the way through. Place them in a pot with the water and salt. Cover and bring to a boil over high heat; reduce heat and simmer for 10 minutes. Drain completely and set aside.

Make a marinade by combining olive oil, vinegar, salt, and sugar in a saucepan, uncovered. Bring to a boil. Reduce heat and simmer for 10 minutes. Remove from heat and add the tarragon, rosemary, onions, garlic, pepper, and allspice.

Place the drained mushrooms in pint size sterilized jars. Slowly pour the marinade over the mushrooms to cover. Allow to cool completely. Cover and store in refrigerator for up to, but not over, one week.

MINT GREEN FRUIT DIP

Refreshing and very different from your run-of-the mill dips, this one lends a cool change and lovely color to your cocktail party or buffet. Both the look and the taste are spectacular. Not for children because of the Crème de Menthe.

Ingredients

1 (6 ounce) container fat free lime yogurt

1 (6 ounce) container fat free plain yogurt

1 tablespoon green Crème de Menthe

Ladyfingers

An assortment of fruit such as fresh whole strawberries, pineapple chunks, honeydew cubes, thick sliced bananas, or pink grapefruit

Several mint leaves

Procedure

Combine the yogurts and Crème de Menthe in a small bowl. Mix until thoroughly blended. Pour into a pretty dip bowl, place in the center of a large platter or plate. Just before serving, surround the dip with fruit and garnish with mint leaves. Place ladyfingers, ready for dipping, on a separate plate, and position next to the platter of fruit. Provide cocktail picks for spearing fruit.

Yield: 1½ cups of dip.

NUTTY GRAPES

Grapes have soluble fiber and antioxidants. Nuts are high in omega-3. The cheese and cream are free of dangerous fat. What a perfect snack or appetizer for those of us watching our cholesterol! Enjoy.

Preheat oven to 350°

Ingredients

1 ½ cups pecans or walnuts, toasted and finely crushed

About 50 grapes, red or green or a combination

4 ounces fat free Yogurt Cheese (see page 50)

2-3 tablespoons fat free half and half cream

Procedure

Spread nuts on a baking sheet and toast in oven for 7-8 minutes or until lightly browned and fragrant. Set aside and let cool. Crush nuts in a nut chopper or seal in a plastic bag and crush with a wooden mallet or the bottom of a small pan.

Whisk together the cheese and enough cream to make a smooth thick paste that will adhere to the grapes. Coat each grape with the cheese mixture, then roll grapes in crushed nuts.

Serve with plenty of toothpicks for spearing.

Feeds about 8-10 people.

RED, WHITE and GREEN PARTY "TRAYS"

A spectacular presentation, colorful and enticing. Serve this as an appetizer at holiday time.

Ingredients

Store bought bottled fat free Italian salad dressing

14 ounce package frozen broccoli florets, thawed

1 tablespoon minced garlic

1 quart cherry tomatoes

1 jar pickled pearl onions

2 loaves round bread

Procedure

Place florets in a bowl, sprinkle with garlic, stir gently. Pour one half of the dressing over all. Stir gently until all florets are coated. Refrigerate.

Place tomatoes in a separate bowl, pour over remaining dressing, stir to coat. Refrigerate.

Drain the onions and place in a third bowl. Refrigerate.

After an hour or so, remove from refrigerator. Spear each vegetable with a cocktail pick and insert the picks into the top the bread loaves, alternating the three colors.

Enough for 20 to 30 people.

ROLL 'em up APPETIZER PLATTER

Ingredients for Turkey Roll

3 tablespoons reduced fat or fat free mayonnaise

1 teaspoon minced sweet onion or ½ teaspoon dried onion flakes

½ pound low fat deli turkey breast, sliced

Arugula

Procedure

Combine mayonnaise and onion. Spread on slice of turkey. Add a layer of arugula, roll up and secure with a cocktail pick.

Ingredients for Ham Roll

2 tablespoons Dijon mustard

1 tablespoon fat free plain yogurt

½ pound low fat, lean deli ham

Curly green lettuce

Procedure

Combine mustard and yogurt, spread on slice of ham. Add lettuce, roll up and secure with a cocktail.

Ingredients for Salmon Roll

3 tablespoons Yogurt Cheese (see page 50) or low fat cream cheese

1 teaspoon finely chopped chives

¼ pound thinly sliced smoked salmon

Watercress

cont...

Procedure

Combine Yogurt Cheese and chives. Spread mixture on salmon, add watercress and secure with a cocktail pick.

Garnish

Cherry or grape tomatoes
Chopped fresh flat leaf parsley

Arrange the roll ups in a spiral design on a round platter, scatter tomatoes throughout, and sprinkle with parsley.

SHRIMP COCKTAIL with LEMON SAUCE

This lemony-peppery dipping sauce is a refreshing change from the usual tomato-based bottled cocktail sauce, often nothing more than jazzed up ketchup. For years shrimp and other shellfish were thought to be high in cholesterol, but recent studies have shown they actually aid in reducing it. See Chapter 1 for more information.

Ingredients

1 ½ pounds prepared jumbo shrimp, chilled
½ cup reduced fat or fat free mayonnaise
½ cup fat free sour cream
1 or 2 teaspoons hot pepper sauce (depending on how spicy you like your sauce)
2 teaspoons lemon pepper seasoning (I like McCormick's)
1 teaspoon freshly squeezed lemon juice
Baby spinach

cont...

Procedure

Combine mayonnaise, sour cream, pepper sauce, seasoning and lemon juice. Refrigerate for 15-20 minutes, allowing flavors to blend. Transfer to a small bowl and place in the center of your best serving platter. Surround the bowl with a bed of baby spinach and arrange shrimp on top.

SNAPPY OLIVES

Ingredients

1 ½ pints green olives, pitted or stuffed

2 cloves garlic, chopped

1 teaspoon crushed red pepper flakes

3 teaspoons dried dill weed

2 bay leaves

5 tablespoons olive oil

5 tablespoons white wine vinegar

Procedure

Drain olives. Combine olives and all ingredients in a Ziploc bag. Marinate for two days in refrigerator.

Serves 8-10.

SPINACH DIP

A robust savory dip, full of flavor with just a bit of bite. This is oh, so good! Spinach provides soluble fiber to help rid our arteries of dangerous plaque.

Ingredients

1 (10 ounce) package frozen chopped spinach, thawed, drained, and squeezed dry

4 ounces water chestnuts, drained and finely chopped

1 ½ cups fat free sour cream

½ cup fat free plain yogurt

½ cup finely chopped scallions or Vidalia onion

¼ teaspoon dried tarragon

½ teaspoon dry mustard

1 clove garlic, minced

Coarse ground pepper to taste

Procedure

Combine all ingredients. Chill one hour or more before serving, allowing the flavors to marry. Serve with sesame rice crackers, baked potato chips, or chunks of French bread.

Yield: 2 cups

STUFFED CHERRY TOMATO APPETIZERS

Ingredients

1 small can lightly salted peanuts

1 box large cherry tomatoes

1 cup Yogurt Cheese (See recipe on page 50)

½ teaspoon dried onions

¼ teaspoon garlic powder

1 teaspoon dried dill

Curly green lettuce

Procedure

Use a nut chopper or place peanuts in a resealable plastic bag and crush with a wooden mallet or the bottom of a small heavy pan. Halve each tomato. Scoop out the insides, leaving the shell intact. Combine Yogurt Cheese, onions, garlic powder, and dill. Place in refrigerator for at least 20 minutes to allow flavors to meld.

Fill tomatoes with the Yogurt Cheese Mixture, mounding up in the centers. Sprinkle each with crushed peanuts. Layer a large platter with lettuce and arrange the stuffed tomatoes on top.

Makes 40-50 halves.

DO AHEAD LEMON YOGURT CHEESE SPREAD

As easy as 1-2-3 to assemble, this piquant tasting little appetizer is cholesterol safe and goes well with crackers or pumpernickel cocktail rounds. You'll love it, also, as a spread on Pumpkin Pie Muffins. (See recipe in the Bread and Muffin section of this book).

Ingredients

8 ounces Yogurt Cheese (See recipe on page 50)

1 teaspoon lemon zest (grated lemon rind)

1 teaspoon freshly squeezed lemon juice

Sugar to taste

Procedure

Combine all ingredients thoroughly. You may make this the day before you plan to serve it and refrigerate. In a hurry? Refrigerate for at least 20 minutes before serving, allowing time for the flavors to blend.

Beverages

CRANBERRY LEMON PUNCH

Festive, bright, delicious, and nutritious! This is a great party punch. If this is being served to adults, you may wish to add 2 cups of vodka.

Ingredients

Fresh cranberries

6 cups cranberry or cranberry apple juice, chilled

12 ounce container frozen lemonade, made according to directions

2 quarts pale dry ginger ale, chilled

Mint leaves

Procedure

To assemble the punch:

Pour chilled cranberry juice and prepared lemonade into a punch bowl. Immediately before serving, add ginger ale for fizz along with ice cubes. Float extra cranberries and mint leaves on top for extra color. Makes about one gallon.

FRESH and FRAGRANT GINGER TEA

This is so much better than anything that comes in a tea bag. It's so good you'll find yourself breathing in its perfume and savoring every sip. Recipe for Nancy's Pumpkin Bread is in the Breads and Muffins section of this book.

cont...

Ingredients

Fresh ginger root
Boiling water

Procedure

Put a kettle of cold water on to boil over high heat. Now "hot the pot" by filling a 6-8 cup teapot with hot water and letting it stand for about one minute. Meanwhile, cut several thin slices of ginger. Empty pot of water and add the ginger. Pour in the boiling water and allow to steep for five minutes. Serve with honey and slices of Nancy's Pumpkin Bread.

HOT APPLE CIDER

Sip this by the fireplace on a cold winter night. Perfect aprés ski drink, served with Chocolate Hazelnut Macaroons. You'll find the recipe for the macaroons under Cookies in the Dessert section of this book.

Ingredients

8 whole cloves
2 quarts apple cider
½ cup sweetened dried cranberries
½ cup dried cherries
3 cinnamon sticks
Extra whole cinnamon sticks

cont...

Procedure

Place the cloves on a small piece of cheese cloth and tie into a small sack. Combine the sack with the apple cider, cranberries, and cherries in a large pot. Heat only to a simmer; do not boil. Break the 3 cinnamon sticks in thirds and add to the pot. Continue to simmer for 3-4 minutes. Remove the cheesecloth sack and discard. Serve in mugs with a cinnamon stick in each.

Serves 8.

MAKE YOUR OWN PEPPERMINT TEA

A good pot of tea needs oxygen. Starting with cold water and bringing it to a rolling boil introduces oxygen into the tea.

Ingredients

4 Earl Grey Tea bags
4 fresh mint leaves
Boiling water

Procedure

Bring a kettle of cold water to a rolling boil. Preheat a 6 cup teapot by filling it with hot tap water and letting it sit for about one minute. Bruise the mint leaves to release flavor by crushing with your fingers. Empty teapot, but do not dry it. Add the teabags and mint leaves and pour in the boiling water. Allow to steep for about five minutes. Stir before serving to distribute the flavors evenly and serve with Lemon Blueberry Cranberry Tea Cakes.

Makes six cups.

Note: Look in the Dessert Section for the Lemon Blueberry Cranberry Tea Cakes.

MIKE'S EXPRESSO MARTINI

Mike Vieira is a mixologist* at Turtle Soup, a well known restaurant in Narragansett, Rhode Island. Here is the recipe for one of his very special martinis. Thank you, Mike!

Ingredients

3 ounces Stoli Vanilla Vodka

3 ounces of Three Olives Triple Shot Expresso Vodka

1 ounce of Kahlua

1 ounce of Bailey's Irish Cream

1 ounce of Crème De Cacao

Splash of Frangelico Liqueur

Procedure

Combine ingredients, shake well, and pour into a 10 ounce martini glass.

* Note: According to Webster's dictionary, a mixologist is one who is skilled in the art of mixed drinks.

MIKE'S VERSION of a PINK LADY

Here is another contribution from Mike Vieira. No saturated fat, no cholesterol, and no trans fat!

cont...

Ingredients

5 ounces Raspberry Stoli
2.5 ounces Cointreau or Triple Sec
1 ounce pomegranate juice
Splash of orange juice

Procedure

Combine ingredients, shake well, and pour.

MIXED BERRY SHRUB

Ingredients

16 ounce package frozen unsweetened mixed berries
3 cups cold water
¼ cup wildflower honey
3 tablespoons balsamic vinegar

Procedure

Place frozen berries in a blender with 3 cups cold water. Process on high until smooth. Add honey and balsamic vinegar and continue to blend until thick and very smooth. Serve immediately or keep chilled in refrigerator. Stir briskly or shake before serving.

Makes 1 ½ to 2 quarts.

PEACH BANANA DESSERT SMOOTHIE

So good, we can call this a drinkable dessert, yet all these ingredients are cholesterol friendly. Cool and refreshing with just the right amount of sweetness.

Ingredients

- 1 ½ cups fresh peach slices (substitute frozen, or canned and drained)
- 1 medium yellow-ripe banana, sliced
- ⅔ cup low fat or fat free peach yogurt (substitute vanilla)
- ⅔ cup non fat peach frozen yogurt (substitute vanilla)
- ⅔ cup orange juice
- 2 mint leaves for garnish

Procedure

Place all ingredients in a large blender or food processor. If you have a small machine, divide and process in two batches. Pulse 2 or 3 times and then blend on high speed until smooth, about 8 or 10 seconds. Scrape sides of machine and blend for 5 seconds more. Pour into tall chilled glasses and garnish with mint leaf on top.

Makes two generous smoothies.

SLUSHY BERRY SHRUB

This thick, bright, and refreshing smoothie is perfect on a hot summer day. The berries make it an ultimate high antioxidant drink. Remember, as a general rule, the brighter a fruit's color, the higher its content of antioxidants.

Ingredients

16 ounces package unsweetened frozen mixed berries

6 tablespoons clover honey

3 tablespoons white balsamic vinegar (brown is fine but will alter the color)

3 cups cold water

Procedure

Place the berries, still frozen, in a blender. Add the cold water, pulse a few times, then process on high speed until smooth. Add the honey and vinegar. Blend until smooth and very thick. Serve immediately or refrigerate. Remove from refrigerator and stir briskly or put in a container with a tight lid and shake before serving.

Makes 6 ½ cups.

SUN TEA PUNCH

This is oh, so pretty and fun to make! Great for entertaining, it makes an impressive presentation. Delicious and refreshing on a hot summer day.

Ingredients

2 quarts cold water

8 Earl Grey (or your favorite) tea bags

2 quarts bottle store bought fruit punch, chilled

2 quarts pale dry ginger ale, chilled

6 whole fresh strawberries

6 strawberries, sliced

Procedure

Pour the water into a large clear glass container, add the teabags, and place in the sun for a few hours or until the color looks like strong tea. Refrigerate. This can be done the day before you plan to serve the punch.

To assemble the punch

Place ice in a large punch bowl. Pour the cold tea and the fruit punch over the ice. Immediately before serving, add the ginger ale for a bit of fizz and float the sliced strawberries on top. Beautiful!

Makes a gallon and a half of punch.

Breads & Muffins

GLAZED CRANBERRY SQUASH BREAD

Here is a quick bread even more tasty than those made with butter or shortening. This offers the added benefits of oatmeal, canola, cinnamon and egg substitute. Eat this with no guilt, knowing that you are helping in your battle against high cholesterol. A great gift, especially around the holidays.

Preheat oven to 350°

Ingredients

3 ½ cups presifted flour

2 teaspoons baking soda

1 tablespoon baking powder

2 tablespoons cinnamon

2 teaspoons nutmeg

2 teaspoons ginger

1 teaspoon ground cloves

1 teaspoon salt

2 ½ cups granulated sugar

1 cup canola oil

2 cups cooked mashed butternut squash

⅔ cup water

8 ounces egg substitute

1 ½ cups quick cooking oatmeal

1 ½ cups dried sweetened cranberries (Craisins)

Canola cooking spray

Small amount of flour

cont...

Procedure

In a large mixing bowl, thoroughly combine flour, baking soda, baking powder, spices, salt, and sugar. Stir in canola, squash, water, and egg substitute. Add oatmeal and cranberries.

Generously coat 3 loaf pans with canola spray and dust lightly with flour. Divide batter among the 3 pans, ½ to ¾ full. Bake about 1 hour and 15 minutes or until a toothpick inserted in the center comes out clean. Place on cooling racks for about 10 minutes. Run a knife around the edges of each loaf to loosen and remove from pans. Serve warm or cool completely, wrap tightly in foil and store in freezer.

GLAZE

Ingredients

4 cups powdered sugar

¾ cup water

1 teaspoon vanilla

Procedure

Combine 1 cup of the sugar with the water in a saucepan. Cook over medium/low heat. Stir until a syrup is formed. The syrup is ready if a thread is formed when a small quantity is dripped from a spoon. Remove from heat and let the syrup cool slightly. Place the remaining 3 cups of powdered sugar in a bowl and add enough syrup to produce a glaze the consistency of heavy cream. Stir in vanilla. Pour over the cooled loaves and let the glaze run down the sides. Glaze sets up in 3 to 4 minutes.

HERB QUICK DINNER ROLLS

Although these "rolls" are baked in a cupcake tin, they resemble cupcakes or muffins in shape only. Their flavor and texture place them in the category of rolls and they are a good accompaniment to a simple meal.

Preheat oven to 400°

Ingredients

1 ¼ cups presifted flour
1 ¼ cups oat bran cereal, uncooked
1 tablespoon baking powder
1 teaspoon baking soda
½ teaspoon celery salt
½ teaspoon sea salt
½ teaspoon black pepper
1 teaspoon minced dried onion
½ teaspoon dried parsley
½ teaspoon dried rosemary
½ teaspoon dried thyme
3 egg whites or two whole extra large eggs
1 cup skim milk
⅓ cup canola oil
1 tablespoon fresh lemon juice
Canola cooking spray

Procedure

In a large mixing bowl thoroughly combine flour, oat bran cereal, baking powder, baking soda, salts, and pepper. Incorporate onion, parsley, rosemary, and thyme. Set aside. In a small bowl,

cont...

beat eggs with a fork until frothy. Add milk, canola oil, and lemon juice. Stir the egg mixture into the dry mix; combine completely but do not beat. Spray each section of a cupcake tin generously with canola oil and fill with batter.

Bake on the middle rack of your oven for 13 minutes. Remove from oven to a rack and let cool for 5 minutes. Run a slim knife around the edge of "rolls" to loosen before removing. Serve warm, or allow to cool completely and store in freezer in an airtight container. Warm frozen rolls briefly in micro wave.

Makes 8-10 dinner rolls.

ITALIAN DINNER ROLLS

An Italian fragrance will fill your kitchen when these are baking. I call these "rolls" even though they are cooked in a cupcake (muffin) pan. They are oh, so good served with simple pasta that has been dressed with a good extra virgin olive oil, salt and pepper and, if your cholesterol is under control, a little fresh grated parmesan cheese.

Preheat oven to 400°

Ingredients

¾ cups presifted flour

1 ¾ cups oat bran cereal, uncooked

1 tablespoon baking powder

1 teaspoon baking soda

½ teaspoon celery salt

½ teaspoon sea salt

½ teaspoon black pepper

½ teaspoon dried basil

cont...

½ teaspoon dried oregano

¼ teaspoon garlic powder

½ teaspoon dried onion flakes

2 large eggs or 3 egg whites

1 cup skim milk

⅓ cup olive oil

Canola cooking spray

Procedure

In a large size mixing bowl, thoroughly combine flour, oat bran, baking powder, baking soda, celery salt, sea salt, pepper, basil, oregano, garlic powder, and onion flakes. In a small bowl, beat eggs with a fork until frothy. Add eggs along with milk and olive oil to oat bran mixture. Stir together by hand. Allow to stand while you generously spray bottom and sides of 10 sections of a muffin pan. Fill each chamber. Bake on middle rack of your oven for 13 minutes. Let cool for 5 minutes before removing from pan. Serve warm from the oven or reheat cooled rolls briefly in a micro wave oven. Refrigerate or freeze in an airtight container.

Makes 10 rolls.

NANCY'S PUMPKIN BREAD

Traditional pumpkin bread recipes include white flour, shortening, and whole eggs. My daughter-in-law Nancy's version offers a highly flavorful and moist bread with the benefit of oatmeal, canola oil, and egg substitute.

Preheat oven to 350°

Ingredients

3 ½ cups whole wheat flour
2 teaspoons baking soda
1 tablespoon baking powder
2-3 tablespoons cinnamon
2-3 teaspoons nutmeg
2-3 teaspoons ginger
2 teaspoons powdered cloves
1 ½ teaspoons salt
2 ½ cups sugar
1 cup canola oil
1 can pumpkin (15 ounce)
⅔ cup water
8 ounces egg substitute
1 ½ cups oatmeal
1 ½ cups raisins
Canola cooking spray

Procedure

In a large bowl, thoroughly combine flour, baking soda, baking powder, spices, salt, and sugar. Stir in canola, pumpkin, water, and egg substitute. Add oatmeal and raisins.

cont...

Generously spray 3 loaf pans with canola oil and dust lightly with flour. Divide batter among the 3 pans (½ to ¾ full). Bake 1 hour and 15 minutes or until a toothpick inserted in the center of each loaf comes out clean.

Allow to cool for 10 minutes before removing from pans.

Nancy Serpa

APPLE RAISIN OAT BRAN MUFFINS

A great tasting muffin that's perfect for breakfast, afternoon tea, or evening snack. The oat bran, cinnamon, and canola oil are all high on my list for cholesterol reducing foods. To add to this, the cholesterol friendly apples and raisins are full of soluble fiber, antioxidants, and vitamins. This has been voted my family's #1 favorite muffin.

Preheat oven to 400°

Ingredients

2 ½ cups oat bran hot cereal (uncooked)

1 tablespoon baking powder

1 teaspoon baking soda

1 ½ teaspoons cinnamon

¼ teaspoon nutmeg

1 tablespoon brown sugar (optional)

½ teaspoon salt

1 cup fat free evaporated milk or 1 cup skim milk

4 ounces egg substitute or 3 egg whites

4 tablespoons canola oil

cont...

½ cup raisins

1 cup chopped apples

Canola spray or foil baking cups

Procedure

Thoroughly combine oat bran, baking powder, baking soda, cinnamon, nutmeg, brown sugar, and salt. Stir in milk, eggs, oil, and raisins. Set aside. Batter will thicken slightly.

Generously spray muffin pan with canola cooking spray or line each chamber with foil baking cups. Fold apples into batter. Spoon batter into cups until almost full. Bake 12-15 minutes. Do not overbake. Let cool for 5 minutes before removing from pan. Store completely cooled muffins in freezer or refrigerator. Warm in microwave before serving.

Yield: 10-12 muffins.

AUTUMN OAT BRAN MUFFINS

These are my very favorite muffins. Bake them when butternut squash is in season. They bake up high and moist, their heavenly aroma reminiscent of Thanksgiving at Grandma's. The oat bran, cinnamon, and canola oil are known to lower cholesterol so, "Over the river and through the woods-----." Enjoy!

Preheat oven to 400°

Ingredients

2 ½ cups oat bran

1 tablespoon baking powder

cont...

1 teaspoon baking soda

1 ½ teaspoons cinnamon

¼ teaspoon ginger

½ teaspoon nutmeg

1 teaspoon salt

¼ cup brown sugar

1 cup fat free skim or canned evaporated milk

3 egg whites

3 tablespoons canola oil

2 cups cooked and mashed fresh or frozen butternut squash (do not use canned squash)

1 cup Craisins (sweetened dried cranberries)

Canola cooking spray or foil

Procedure

Mix together thoroughly the oat bran, baking powder, baking soda, cinnamon, ginger, nutmeg, salt, and sugar. Add milk, egg whites, and canola oil. Let the batter stand for five minutes, allowing the oat bran to absorb moisture. Meanwhile, prepare a muffin pan, either lining the chambers with foil cups or generously spraying bottom and sides with canola cooking spray. Set aside. Back to the batter, which by now has thickened. Stir in the squash and cranberries, combining well. Fill muffin chambers. Bake 12-14 minutes or until a toothpick, inserted in the center comes out clean. *Do not overbake or muffins will be dry.*

Yield: 12 muffins.

BANANA NUT MUFFINS

If you've been accustomed to store bought muffins, you'll find these so much better. Commercial muffins are often made with lard which Webster describes as "a soft white solid or semisolid fat made by rendering fatty pork." Sounds pretty yucky! They usually contain far too much sugar and sometimes taste more like cupcakes than muffins.

Preheat oven to 400°

Ingredients

1 ½ cups uncooked oat bran hot cereal

½ cup light brown sugar

½ teaspoon sea salt

1 cup presifted flour

1 tablespoon baking powder

1 teaspoon baking soda

1 cup skim milk

3 egg whites

2 tablespoons fresh lemon juice

1 teaspoon vanilla

¼ cup canola oil

2 large or three small very ripe bananas, mashed

½ cup chopped walnuts

Canola cooking spray or additional canola oil

Flour

Procedure

Thoroughly combine cereal, sugar, salt, flour, baking powder, and baking soda. Stir in milk, egg whites, lemon juice, vanilla,

cont...

and oil, mixing only until moistened. Add bananas and nuts.

Very generously coat each chamber of a muffin pan with canola spray or regular canola oil. Dust lightly with flour. Spoon in the batter. Bake 13-15 minutes. Do not overbake. Let cool for 10 minutes before removing from pan.

Yield: 12 muffins.

BLUEBERRY MUFFINS

These muffins need no sugar. If you have a sweet tooth and simply must have extra sweetness, add 1 or 2 tablespoons of brown sugar to the dry ingredients. Besides being delicious, they have cholesterol fighting ingredients (canola oil, oat bran, cinnamon). Eggs and milk add protein and remember, blueberries are high on the list of antioxidants.

Preheat oven to 400°

Ingredients

2 ½ cups oat bran hot cereal, uncooked
1 tablespoon baking powder
1 teaspoon baking soda
1 teaspoon cinnamon
¼ teaspoon nutmeg
½ teaspoon salt (optional)
¼ cup canola oil
3 extra large egg whites
1 cup skimmed milk
1 cup fresh blueberries
Canola cooking spray or foil cupcake liners

cont...

Procedure

Thoroughly combine cereal, baking powder, baking soda, cinnamon, nutmeg, and salt. Add canola oil, eggs, and milk. Mix well but do not beat. Set aside. (Batter will thicken slightly on standing.)

Generously spray bottom and sides of each muffin pan chamber or line with foil cups. Gently fold blueberries into the batter. Fill each unit to the top and bake for 12 to 14 minutes, being careful not to overbake. The tops should be crusty but not brown. Allow to cool in pan for 5 minutes. Serve warm or cool completely and store in an airtight container, placing in your refrigerator for up to one week or in the freezer for up to 2 months.

Makes 10 to 12 muffins.

"The hostess must be like the duck-calm and unruffled on the surface, and paddling like hell underneath."

—Anonymous

CARROT CAKE MUFFINS

This may look like a long list of ingredients, but the recipe goes together quickly. Oat bran, cinnamon, and canola are all cholesterol reducing. Added benefits are derived from the vitamins and minerals found in the carrots and raisins. Eggs and milk contribute protein. Carrots, when cooked, produce beta carotene. Super healthy and great tasting!

Preheat oven to 400°

Ingredients

2 ½ cups uncooked oat bran hot cereal

1 tablespoon baking powder

1 teaspoon baking soda

1 teaspoon salt (optional)

1 ½ teaspoons cinnamon

¼ teaspoon nutmeg

⅛ teaspoon ginger

2 tablespoons brown sugar

1 cup skimmed milk or canned fat free evaporated milk

3 egg whites or 4 ounces egg substitute

⅓ cup canola oil

1 cup loosely packed grated carrots

¾ cup raisins

Canola baking spray or foil baking cups

cont...

Procedure

Mix together oat bran, baking powder, baking soda, salt, cinnamon, nutmeg, ginger, and brown sugar, being certain the spices are well combined.

Add milk, eggs, canola, carrots, and raisins. Generously coat muffin pan with canola spray or line with foil cupcake liners. Fill each chamber to the top and bake for 13-15 minutes. I find that placing the pan on the middle rack of my oven works best. Careful not to overbake! Overcooking will produce dry, dense muffins. The tops should be crusty but not brown. Allow to cool for five minutes before removing from pan. Serve warm or let cool completely and store in an airtight container in refrigerator or freezer. Frozen muffins will usually thaw in ten minutes or can be micro waved for 20-25 seconds, depending on your oven.

Yield: 12 muffins

CRANBERRY MANDARIN ORANGE MUFFINS

You will gain points with these delectable muffins. The oat bran and canola have been proven to help reduce cholesterol, the two fruits are cholesterol friendly and give you the added benefit of being high in antioxidants, soluble fiber, and vitamin C. As with all my muffin recipes, it is important not to overbake in order to keep them moist and light.

Preheat oven to 400°

Ingredients

  2 ½ cups uncooked oat bran hot cereal

  1 tablespoon baking powder

  1 teaspoon baking soda

cont...

⅛ teaspoon cloves

1 ½ teaspoons cinnamon

½ teaspoon salt

1 cup skim milk or fat free evaporated

3 egg whites

4 tablespoons canola oil

½ cup Craisins (sweetened dried cranberries)

1 cup drained mandarin oranges

Canola baking spray or foil cupcake liners

Procedure

Thoroughly combine the oat bran, baking powder, baking soda, cloves, cinnamon, and salt. Stir in milk, egg whites, and canola oil. Add the cranberries and set aside. The batter will thicken slightly on standing.

Generously spray each chamber of a muffin pan or line with foil cupcake liners.

Stir in the mandarin oranges. No need to chop them; they will come apart slightly as you incorporate them. Bake for 12 to 14 minutes or until slightly crusty on top, but not brown. Place on a cooling rack and let stand for 5 minutes before removing from pan. Store completely cooled leftover muffins in an airtight container in refrigerator or freezer. Warm in microwave before serving.

Jeannie Serpa

LEMON BLUEBERRY OAT BRAN MUFFINS

Almost everyone loves blueberry muffins. The hint of lemon in these marries well with the blueberries. These refreshing muffins are perfect for breakfast or afternoon tea and children love them! Three important ingredients—canola oil, cinnamon, and oat bran—supply cholesterol lowering benefits AND blueberries are very high in antioxidants!

Preheat oven to 400°

Ingredients

2 cups oat bran hot cereal, uncooked
1 tablespoon baking powder
1 teaspoon baking soda
1 ½ teaspoons cinnamon
¼ cup brown sugar
1 teaspoon salt (optional)
1 cup fat free evaporated milk or skim milk
3 tablespoons canola oil
4 ounces egg substitute or 3 egg whites
¼ cup fat free lemon yogurt
1 tablespoon fresh lemon juice
1 cup fresh blueberries (or frozen blueberries, thawed and drained)
Canola cooking spray or foil baking cups

Procedure

Thoroughly combine oat bran, baking powder, baking soda, cinnamon, sugar, and salt.

Add milk, oil, eggs, yogurt, and lemon juice. Set aside. Batter

cont...

will thicken on standing.

Meanwhile, spray muffin pan generously with canola spray or line with foil baking cups.

Gently fold blueberries into batter and spoon into prepared muffin pan, almost filling each chamber. Bake 13-15 minutes, being careful not to overbake. Let stand 5 minutes before removing from pan. Store completely cooled muffins in refrigerator or freezer.

Yield: 10 muffins.

PINEAPPLE PECAN MUFFINS

If you desire a lighter muffin, you will love these. Some of the oat bran has been replaced with presifted flour, making them less dense. Studies have proved that cinnamon, canola, and pecans actually help to reduce cholesterol. In addition to all that, these are delicious! Add brown sugar only if you like your muffins sweet.

Preheat oven to 400°

Ingredients

1½ cups uncooked oat bran hot cereal

½ cup flour

1 tablespoon baking powder

1 teaspoon baking soda

1½ teaspoons cinnamon

¼ cup brown sugar (optional)

½ teaspoon salt (optional)

1 cup skim milk or fat free evaporated milk

3 egg whites or 4 ounces egg substitute

cont...

3 tablespoons canola oil

1 cup canned, drained pineapple tidbits (reserve ¼ cup juice)

¼ cup coarsely chopped pecans

Canola baking spray or foil baking cups

Procedure

Mix oat bran, flour, baking powder, baking soda, cinnamon, sugar, and salt until well combined. Add milk, eggs, and oil. Combine well but do not beat. Gently fold in pineapple, add reserved juice and pecans. Coat each chamber of muffin pan generously with canola cooking spray or line with foil cups. Spoon batter into cups until almost full. Bake 12 to 15 minutes. Do not overbake. Let stand 5 minutes before removing from pan. Store completely cooled muffins in refrigerator or freezer. Warm frozen muffins in microwave oven. Microwave ovens vary. Start by testing for 20 seconds.

Yield: 10 to 12 muffins

PUMPKIN PIE MUFFINS

Your kitchen will smell like pumpkin pie when these are baking. They are moist and light and rise up beautifully. No saturated fat or trans fat here. Cholesterol reducing ingredients include the oat bran and canola with an added bonus of vitamin A from the pumpkin. And didn't our grandmothers espouse the virtues of molasses? Try these.

Preheat oven to 400°

cont...

Ingredients

2 ½ cups uncooked oat bran hot cereal

1 teaspoon baking soda

1 tablespoon baking powder

1 teaspoon salt

1 tablespoon pumpkin pie spice

2 tablespoons brown sugar

½ can prepared pumpkin (1 cup)

3 egg whites

½ cup fat free half and half cream

½ cup skim milk

¼ cup canola oil

⅛ cup molasses

Canola baking spray or foil cupcake liners

Flour

Procedure

Thoroughly combine oat bran, baking soda, baking powder, salt, pumpkin pie spice, and brown sugar. Add pumpkin, eggs, cream, milk, canola, and molasses. Mix well, but do not beat.

Spray muffin pans with canola and lightly coat with flour. If you choose, simply line with foil baking cups. Fill each chamber to the top. Bake for 12 to 14 minutes. Caution: do not overbake. They are done when crusty on top but not brown.

Makes 12 muffins.

cont...

PUMPKIN, PINEAPPLE, PECAN MUFFINS

Four of the ingredients used here have been proven to actually reduce cholesterol: oat bran, cinnamon, canola, and pecans. In addition, everything else in this recipe is free of the "bad" fats. Here is an ideal muffin for those of us working to keep that cholesterol level down. There's a bonus here, also. They are scrumptious!

Preheat oven to 400°

Ingredients

2 ¼ cups uncooked oat bran hot cereal
1 ½ teaspoons cinnamon
½ teaspoon nutmeg
¼ teaspoon ginger
1 tablespoon baking powder
1 teaspoon baking soda
½ can (1 cup) pumpkin
3 tablespoons canola oil
¼ cup molasses
¾ cup fat free evaporated milk
3 egg whites
1 (8 ounce) can crushed pineapple, with juice
¼ cup chopped pecans
Canola baking spray or foil baking cups

Procedure

Thoroughly mix together oat bran, cinnamon, nutmeg, ginger, baking powder, and baking soda. Add pumpkin, oil, molasses, milk, and eggs. Combine well, then fold in pineapple and

cont...

pecans. Generously spray each chamber of a muffin pan or line with foil cupcake liners. Fill each section to the top and bake for 13-15 minutes, being sure not to overbake.

Yield: 12-15 muffins.

RASPBERRY SURPRISE MUFFINS

At first glance these appear to be plain oat bran muffins until you bite into them. The jam disperses throughout the muffin, adding a sweet flavorful surprise to every bite.

Preheat oven to 400°

Ingredients

2 ½ cups oat bran hot cereal, uncooked

1 tablespoon baking powder

1 teaspoon baking soda

1 ½ teaspoons cinnamon

½ teaspoon nutmeg

Pinch of ginger

½ teaspoon sea salt

3 egg whites or 4 ounces egg substitute

1 cup skim milk

¼ cup canola oil

Raspberry or your favorite jam

Canola cooking spray or foil cups

cont...

Procedure

Thoroughly combine cereal, baking powder, baking soda, cinnamon, nutmeg, ginger, and sea salt. Whip egg whites with a fork until slightly frothy and add to dry ingredients along with the milk and oil. Mix until well combined but do not beat.

Generously coat muffin pan with cooking spray or line with foil cups. Fill each chamber half full with batter then add one heaping teaspoonful of jam. Fill each chamber to the top with additional batter. Bake 12-14 minutes, until tops of muffins are crusty but not browned. Do not overbake. Allow to cool in pan for five minutes before removing. Serve warm or cool completely and store in an airtight container in refrigerator for up to one week or in freezer for up to 2 months.

Makes 10-12 muffins.

"Spaghetti can be eaten most successfully if you inhale it like a vacuum cleaner."

—Sophia Loren

TRIPLE A SUPER MUFFINS

The three A's, Apples, Applesauce, and Apple juice concentrate provide great flavor here. Three important ingredients: oat bran, cinnamon, and canola oil are known to reduce cholesterol. Add to that the vitamins, pectin, and soluble fiber found in apples and you have a superior muffin. Super healthy, super delicious!

Preheat oven to 400°

Ingredients

2 ½ cups oat bran cereal

1 tablespoon baking powder

1 teaspoon baking soda

1 ½ teaspoons cinnamon

½ teaspoon nutmeg

½ teaspoon salt (optional)

1 cup skim or fat free evaporated milk

3 egg whites or 4 ounces egg substitute

4 tablespoons canola oil

¼ cup apple juice concentrate, thawed

¼ cup applesauce

1 teaspoon grated lemon zest

1 large apple, chopped (about 1 and ½ cups)

Canola cooking spray or foil cups

Procedure

Combine thoroughly the oat bran, baking powder, baking soda, cinnamon, nutmeg, and salt. Add milk, eggs, oil, apple concentrate, apple sauce, lemon zest, and chopped apple. Mix

cont...

completely, but do not beat. Generously coat bottom and sides of muffin pan with canola baking spray or line with foil cups. Spoon batter into chambers until almost full.

Bake 12-15 minutes. Do NOT overbake.

Allow to cool on a wire rack for five minutes before removing from pan. Enjoy them warm or place completely cooled muffins in an airtight container and store in the freezer.

Warm in microwave 20 seconds, testing first, since microwave ovens do vary.

Yield: 10-12 muffins.

Salads

BROCCOLI CASHEW SALAD

Ingredients

1 pound baby broccoli florets, fresh or frozen

Salt to taste (optional)

½ cup fat free sour cream

1 tablespoon sugar

½ cup cashew halves

Procedure

Add fresh or still frozen florets to boiling salted water for 60 seconds. Remove, drain and plunge into ice water to set color and retain crispness. Drain again. In a small bowl, whisk sugar into sour cream. Combine well, being sure the sugar has a chance to dissolve. Pour over the florets, toss gently and fold in cashews.

BROCCOLI SLAW

Ordinary slaws are usually bland in color, but here is one that sings with bright green, red, and orange ingredients. Its interesting combination of texture and crunchiness, combined with a perfect blending of sweet and tart flavors, place it high on my list of dinner party side dishes. Serve this with seafood, chicken, or turkey.

Ingredients

1 cup dried sweetened cranberries (Craisins)

½ cup Canadian bacon

½ cup slivered almonds

cont...

½ cup fat free or reduced fat mayonnaise

½ cup canola oil

2 tablespoons white wine vinegar

3 tablespoons granulated sugar

2 heads broccoli

Preparation

Cover cranberries with hot water to soak. Set aside. In a dry skillet, cook bacon over medium heat for 2 minutes. Remove from heat, chop, and set aside. Toast almonds by placing in a dry skillet over medium heat. Cook 5 to 10 minutes or until golden brown and fragrant. Set aside to cool.

Procedure

Mix the dressing by combining mayonnaise, canola oil, vinegar, and sugar. Set aside. Wash broccoli, drain, and cut off florets. Save the stems for another use, if desired. Drain cranberries and combine in a bowl with florets, almonds, onion, carrots, and chopped bacon. Spread on a platter and cover with dressing.

Serves 4 to 6.

CHRISTMAS PEAR SALAD

Festive looking and delicious, this red and green fruit salad is not limited to Christmas. Serve it year round. This is a family tradition started by my sister, Nancy Carroll Cole, many years ago. Quick and easy to make and special enough for a party, here's a dish with no saturated fats or cholesterol, so go for it! (It's also great as a dessert).

Ingredients

1 (6 ounce) package lime Jell-O
1 large can (29 ounces) pear halves
Red maraschino cherries

Procedure

Make Jell-O following directions on box. Pour into a 9x13 inch glass baking dish or large shallow casserole dish. Refrigerate until slightly thickened but not completely set (about 8 minutes). Drain the pears and cherries. Position the pears cut side up in the Jell-O with a bright red cherry nestled in center of each. Return to refrigerator until completely jelled.

CITRUS WINTER SALAD

Citrus fruits are not only plentiful during the winter months but they are at their flavorful best. Use tangerines, grapefruit, clementines, or oranges in this refreshing winter salad. Lots of vitamin C here AND olive oil and avocado have both been proven to help reduce cholesterol.

cont...

Ingredients

¼ cup balsamic vinegar

1 tablespoon honey

½ teaspoon coarse ground black pepper

½ cup extra virgin olive oil

1 head romaine lettuce, washed and chopped

1 tangerine

1 pink grapefruit

1 orange or clementine

1 avocado

¼ cup red onion, finely chopped

Procedure

For the dressing: vigorously whisk together vinegar, honey, pepper, and olive oil. Set aside.

To assemble the salad, peel and section the fruit, removing any pith (the spongy white tissue which lines the rind of most citrus fruits). Plop the romaine in a large salad bowl, sprinkle with the onion and place the fruit sections on top. Cut the avocado in half and remove the pit. Now slice into sections, leaving the skin intact, and scoop out the flesh with a spoon. Arrange the sections over the salad. Give the dressing another vigorous whisk, drizzle the dressing over the salad, and serve immediately. Assemble just before serving. (Avocado tends to turn brown when exposed to oxygen. If serving time must be delayed, sprinkle with lemon juice to prevent oxidation).

Yield: 6-8 servings.

COLORFUL CABBAGE SLAW

A colorful and crunchy slaw, full of soluble fiber, which is so beneficial toward lowering cholesterol. This is not meant to be a creamy slaw and is, therefore, devoid of any harmful saturated fat. If you simply must have a creamy coleslaw, add a little reduced fat mayonnaise to the sugar, vinegar, and lemon juice.

Ingredients

2 tablespoons sugar

¼ cup white vinegar

¼ cup fresh lemon juice

1 small head green cabbage, shredded

2 stalks celery, chopped

¼ cup grated carrots

¼ cup chopped fresh parsley

½ green bell pepper, chopped small

½ red bell pepper, chopped small

¼ cup radishes, sliced

Procedure

In a small bowl, whisk together sugar, vinegar, and lemon juice. Set aside. In a large bowl place cabbage, celery, carrots, parsley, red and green peppers. Sprinkle with salt and toss lightly. Add dressing and refrigerate until ready to serve. Immediately before serving, add the radishes and toss again.

Makes 8-10 servings.

Jeannie Serpa

FANCY FRUIT SALAD

A creamy, cool, and colorful dessert, this is a delightful change from the usual fruit salad. Spoon into in your prettiest stemware and garnish each serving with a cherry and a sprig of mint.

Ingredients

1 (11 ounce) can pineapple chunks

1 (11 ounce) can mandarin oranges

2 bananas, peeled and sliced

½ cup fat free Cool Whip*

¼ cup fat free sour cream

6 red maraschino cherries

Fresh mint leaves

Procedure

Drain pineapple and oranges. Combine Cool Whip and sour cream in a bowl and gently fold in pineapple, oranges, and bananas. Chill in refrigerator for at least one hour. Garnish with cherry and mint.

Serves 6.

Note: Remember to use Cool Whip for special treats only and always in moderation. See Chapter 1: Safe Foods

FRUIT SALAD with RASPBERRY YOGURT DRESSING

Here's a salad that's high in soluble fiber and antioxidants; a combination of fruits enhanced by the perfect dressing.

Ingredients

½ cantaloupe, cut in bite size cubes

½ honeydew melon, cut in bite size cubes

1 pint fresh strawberries, hulled and sliced

1 small bunch green grapes, halved

½ pint fresh blueberries

6 ounce container fat free plain yogurt

2 tablespoons skim milk

1 heaping teaspoon seedless raspberry jam

Mint leaves for garnish (optional)

Procedure

Combine cut up fruit in a large bowl. Whisk together yogurt, milk, and jam.

Spoon fruit into dessert bowls and drizzle with dressing. Garnish with mint, if desired. Serve any extra dressing on the side.

GARBANZO SALAD

Here is a salad that supplies protein (from the garbanzo beans) and plenty of Vitamin A and C (from the vegetables). Cholesterol lowering benefits are derived from both the beans and olive oil, making this a healthful and tasty salad. Great luncheon dish!

Ingredients

1 can garbanzo beans (sometimes called chickpeas)

1 pound fresh or frozen cut green beans, cooked

¼ cup finely chopped sweet onion

2 tablespoons extra virgin olive oil

2 tablespoons fresh lemon juice

1 tablespoon chopped fresh basil or ¼ teaspoon dried

¼ teaspoon dried oregano

Celery salt to taste

Red pepper flakes to taste

¼ teaspoon McCormick's Garlic Seasoning

½ carrot, shredded

Procedure

Rinse garbanzo beans in cold water, drain. Combine with cooked green beans and onion.

Add the next five ingredients and mix well. Chill and allow flavors to "marry." For added color and nutrition, top with shredded carrots.

GOLDEN GLOW GELATIN SALAD

Oh, so pretty and great tasting, here is a salad that couldn't be better for the cholesterol conscious. Jell-O is fat free, as are pineapple and lettuce with their added fringe benefit of vitamins. And we know nuts are invaluable when it comes to reducing cholesterol. So, feel safe and enjoy!

Ingredients

⅞ cup pineapple juice

⅞ cup cold water

½ teaspoon salt

1 package (3 ounce) lemon Jell-O

2 cups grated carrots

1 cup well drained crushed pineapple

½ cup chopped pecans or walnuts

Lettuce of choice

Reduced fat mayonnaise (optional)

Procedure

In a small saucepan, bring pineapple juice, water, and salt to a boil. Add gelatin and stir until dissolved. Chill until thickened but not completely set. Stir in carrots, drained pineapple, and nuts. Turn into a wet 5 or 6 cup mold and place in refrigerator, chilling until firm. Unmold onto a lettuce lined platter. If you are feeling comfortable with your cholesterol level, serve with a small dollop of reduced fat mayonnaise. As an alternative to a molded salad, turn the gelatin mixture into a casserole dish or a 9x13 inch baking dish and allow to chill until firm. Spoon servings onto a salad plate that has been lined with lettuce.

Serves 8.

GREEN and GOLD SALAD

A full flavored combination of romaine and fruit, this salad is further enhanced by the orange dressing. Free of dangerous fats and cholesterol, it is the perfect salad for cholesterol watchers who have grown bored with the usual iceberg, tomatoes, and cucumbers. Too often, seeking more flavor, we drown the latter in high fat bottled dressings.

Ingredients

⅔ cup canola oil

⅓ cup orange juice

3 tablespoons white wine vinegar

1 small clove garlic

1 ½ tablespoons orange zest (grated orange peel)

1 ½ teaspoons basil

½ teaspoon granulated sugar

½ teaspoon salt

Dash pepper

1 ½ heads romaine

3 oranges, peeled and sectioned

2 avocados, peeled and sliced thick

Procedure

At least 1¼ hours before serving time prepare the orange dressing: Place oil, orange juice, vinegar, garlic, orange zest, basil, sugar, salt, and pepper in a blender. Cover and blend on low speed until well combined. Pour into a covered container and refrigerate to chill and allow flavors to marry.

At serving time, tear bite size pieces of romaine directly into a salad bowl. Add orange sections and avocado slices. Toss gently with ¾ cup of the dressing until well coated.

Serves 8-12.

HEIRLOOM TOMATO SALAD

Heirloom tomatoes have a short summer season, so grab them when available. They are absolutely the best for full flavor and bright color. This is a salad that is beautiful to behold and deliciously unique with its simple honey dressing.

Ingredients

1 red Heirloom tomato

1 orange Heirloom tomato

1 yellow Heirloom tomato

Baby spinach

Fresh ground black pepper

Honey

Procedure

Cut each tomato into thick slices (about ¼ inch). On a bed of baby spinach, arrange a spiral of tomatoes, alternating the three colors. Sprinkle black pepper over all and drizzle on the honey.

Serves 4.

LETTUCE WEDGES with MAKE BELIEVE MAYO

I'm not about to claim that this mayonnaise tastes like the real thing, but it is an extremely tasty spread that you'll enjoy in sandwiches, on salads, or as a dip with celery and carrot sticks. Real mayonnaise can contain as much as 1.5 grams of saturated fat per serving of 2 table-spoons. This version has none whatsoever. Give it a try. Those grams add up!

cont...

Ingredients

1 head iceberg lettuce

¾ cup Make Believe Mayo

1 tablespoon fresh parsley, finely chopped

Paprika

Procedure

Remove outer layer of lettuce and the core. Cut into single serving size wedges, one to a plate. Just before serving, drizzle with Make Believe Mayo, sprinkle with parsley, and dust with a little paprika.

Serves 6-8, depending on size of iceberg head.

MAKE BELIEVE MAYO

Ingredients

6 ounce container fat free plain yogurt

2 tablespoon fat free lemon yogurt

Paprika

Black pepper

Procedure

Combine the two yogurts. Add a pinch of paprika for color and a dash or two of black pepper for additional flavor. This will keep in your refrigerator for as long as the expiration date on the containers.

Makes ¾ of a cup.

cont...

LORI'S BLACK BEAN and CORN SALAD

Lori Faragalli is executive chef at West Bay Gourmet, a perfectly charming restaurant on Route 1-A in Narragansett, R.I. Known for her healthy dishes, here is just one of Lori's best. This scrumptious recipe has many cholesterol reducing ingredients. At the top of the list: beans, followed by olive oil and all those fresh vegetables and herbs.

Ingredients

1 cup olive oil

¼ cup apple cider vinegar

2 tablespoons honey

1 tablespoon chili powder

1 tablespoon cumin

½ teaspoon salt

¼ teaspoon black pepper

1 (15.5 ounce) can black beans, drained and rinsed in cold water

1 package frozen corn kernels

¼ cup green bell pepper, cut into small dice

1 red pepper, cut into small dice

1 small jalapeno pepper, also small dice

2 scallions, chopped

2 tablespoons chopped fresh parsley

1 tablespoon chopped fresh cilantro

Mixed greens or baby spinach

cont...

117

Procedure

To make the dressing, whisk together olive oil, apple cider vinegar, honey, chili powder, cumin, salt, and pepper.

Place beans and corn in a medium size bowl. Pour dressing over both and stir to combine. Add all 3 peppers, scallions, parsley, and cilantro. Let stand 10 minutes, allowing flavors to marry. Serve over mixed greens or baby spinach as a light lunch or as an accompaniment to grilled chicken.

MARINATED ASPARAGUS SALAD

Looking for a salad that will wow your guests? This impressive salad is a touch above the ordinary, making it perfect for special occasions. Take advantage of asparagus in season when prices are low and flavor is high. The asparagus can be cooked and marinated ahead of time. Its final assembly can be left until the last minute. A delicious and colorful accompaniment to fish, chicken, or turkey.

Ingredients

2 pounds asparagus

3 tablespoons olive oil

2 tablespoons lemon juice

About 4 cups of mesculin (sometimes called spring or baby) greens

Cherry tomatoes, halved

Procedure

Wash the asparagus and snap off the ends where they break easily. Steam or simmer in water until tender crisp. Combine olive oil and lemon juice.

cont...

Drain the asparagus, then marinate in half the olive oil and lemon mix.

Allow to cool, and refrigerate until ready to use.

Distribute the greens evenly on a large platter, piling the asparagus neatly in the center.

Surround with tomato halves, cut side down, and drizzle over all with remaining oil and lemon.

6-8 generous servings.

MELON COMPOTE

Whether you choose to serve this colorful compote for breakfast with muffins or as a light dessert with cookies, you'll find it cool, refreshing, and cholesterol friendly.

Ingredients

1 ½ cups chilled watermelon, seeded and cubed
1 ½ cups chilled cantaloupe, cubed
1 ½ cups chilled honeydew melon, cubed
2 tablespoons honey
3 tablespoons fresh lemon juice
1 tablespoon finely chopped mint leaves
Extra mint leaves for garnish

cont...

Procedure

Combine watermelon, cantaloupe, and honeydew melon in a medium size bowl. Stir honey, lemon juice, and mint together. Pour over the fruit and toss very gently to coat.

Refrigerate until ready to serve. Garnish with mint leaves.

Makes 4 servings.

ORANGE SALAD

This can be served on a bed of curly lettuce as a cool refreshing fruit salad, or as a dessert. For dessert, spoon into your prettiest stemware and finish off with a sprinkling of crushed walnuts.

Ingredients

1 small carton fat free small curd cottage cheese

1 small (3 ounce) box orange Jell-O

1 can (20 ounces) crushed pineapple, drained

1 jar (24.5 ounces or equivalent) mandarin oranges, drained

1 small tub (8 ounces) fat free Cool Whip, thawed

Procedure

Thoroughly combine the cottage cheese and dry Jell-O. Completely drain the pineapple and the oranges. Add the fruits to the cheese mixture. Gently fold in the Cool Whip*.

Spoon into a casserole dish. Refrigerate for one hour or more, allowing flavors to combine.

Serves 6 to 8.

* *Note: Remember to use Cool Whip for special treats only and always in moderation. See Chapter 1: Safe Foods*

RADICCHIO CABBAGE SLAW

Although radicchio looks like a small head of red cabbage, it is actually a member of the chicory family and is sweeter and more tender than cabbage. Here is a salad which, when combined with the pineapple and walnuts, gives us a great tasting slaw that is high in soluble fiber and omega-3, two of our best cholesterol fighters.

Ingredients

2 heads radicchio, shredded

1 head green cabbage, shredded

Sea salt

½ cup fat free or reduced fat mayonnaise

2 teaspoons apple cider vinegar

1 teaspoon granulated sugar

½ cup canned drained pineapple tidbits or ¾ cup drained pineapple chunks (reserve juice)

1 tablespoon pineapple juice

Coarse ground black pepper

¼ cup chopped walnuts

Procedure

Place radicchio and cabbage in a large bowl and sprinkle with salt to taste. Set aside. Whisk together mayonnaise, vinegar, sugar, pineapple, tidbits, juice and black pepper. Pour the dressing over the radicchio and cabbage. Toss lightly and refrigerate until ready to serve. Slaw will become creamier on standing. Sprinkle with nuts just before serving.

Yield: 8-10 servings.

SAVORY COLESLAW

This makes a softer coleslaw than the usual crunchy type and imparts an interesting texture and slightly sweet flavor. Slivered almonds work well here rather than sliced, and lend a bit of crunchiness along with omega-3. The cranberries add bright color and antioxidants. Perfect for those who don't care for traditional coleslaw.

Ingredients

1 head Savoy cabbage, thinly sliced

Sea salt

½ cup reduced or fat free mayonnaise

1 tablespoon honey

1 tablespoon drained sweet relish

¼ teaspoon fresh ground black pepper

¼ cup finely chopped Vidalia or other sweet onion

1 cup sweetened dried cranberries (Craisins)

¼ cup canned slivered almonds

Procedure

Place cabbage in a large bowl and sprinkle with salt. Combine mayonnaise, honey, relish, black pepper, onion, and cranberries. Toss with cabbage and place in refrigerator. The salt will bring out more moisture and the slaw will become creamier on standing. Place the almonds in a dry skillet over medium heat and toast for 5 to 10 minutes or until golden and fragrant. Set aside to cool. Immediately before serving, toss in the almonds.

Yield: 6-8 servings.

SUNSHINE SALAD

Every ingredient in this gelatin salad is cholesterol friendly. It really does look like sunshine with its yellow and orange colors. If you don't have a mold (or don't care to use one), an alternative is to simply pour the gelatin mixture into a casserole dish or a 9x13 inch baking dish and chill until set. Spoon out onto lettuce lined salad plates.

Ingredients

1 package (3 ounce) lemon Jell-O
1 cup hot water
½ cup pineapple juice
½ cup cold water
1 tablespoon vinegar
¼ teaspoon salt
¼ cup grated carrots
1 cup grated cabbage, salted to taste
Curly lettuce or mixed greens

Procedure

Dissolve lemon Jell-O in hot water. Stir in pineapple juice, cold water, vinegar, and salt. Chill until slightly thickened. Remove from refrigerator and add carrots and cabbage.

Pour into a 5 or 6 cup wet mold. Chill until firm. Unmold onto a lettuce lined platter.

THREE BEAN and
ROASTED RED PEPPER SALAD

A super delicious "prepare ahead" salad that's different from the usual fare. Perfect for picnics and tailgating, it carries well. Just pack the lettuce separately and arrange on site. Check labels on bottled dressings carefully. There are now many on the market that are free of saturated and trans fat and fortunately for us, cholesterol friendly.

Preheat oven to 425°

Ingredients

1 large red bell pepper, seeded and cut to large dice

1 large orange bell pepper, seeded and cut to large dice

2 or 3 tablespoons extra virgin olive oil

1 pound fresh green beans, cooked, drained, and cooled

½ pound yellow (wax) beans, cooked, drained, and cooled

1 can black beans, rinsed in cold water and drained

¼ cup low fat Italian bottled dressing

1 head curly green lettuce

8 or 10 cherry tomatoes, halved

Procedure

Spread peppers on a cookie sheet and drizzle with olive oil. Roast for 25 minutes or until crispy tender. Remove from oven. Transfer to a plate and allow to cool. In a large bowl, combine all the beans with the peppers. Drizzle on the Italian dressing and toss gently. Taste test and add more dressing if needed. Mound the salad on a lettuce lined platter and garnish with tomato halves.

Serves 6-8.

THREE GREEN SALAD
with DIJON VINAIGRETTE

Variety of texture and color are evident in this unusual but simple salad combination. Lettuces, olive oil, and nuts all work to help lower your cholesterol.

Ingredients

1 head endive

1 head romaine lettuce

1 head frisée lettuce

¼ cup extra virgin olive oil

1 teaspoon Dijon mustard

2 tablespoons freshly squeezed lemon juice

1 teaspoon honey

2 tablespoons chopped parsley

2 tablespoons rough chopped roasted cashew nuts

Procedure

Chop all lettuces into a large salad bowl and mix just enough to distribute the three varieties evenly. Whisk together olive oil, mustard, lemon juice, and honey. Pour dressing over the greens and toss. Scatter parsley and cashews on top.

Serves 10-12 as a side dish; 4-6 as luncheon plate.

WALDORF PEAR SALAD

My updated rendition of the Waldorf Salad made famous by New York's Waldorf Astoria Hotel in 1902. Seldom seen on menus these days, its history makes it a conversation piece. This is minus the high cholesterol mayonnaise used with the traditional rendition. Pears instead of apples lend a new twist. Great company dish.

Ingredients

2 tablespoons walnut pieces

3 tablespoons olive oil

1 tablespoon apple cider vinegar or fresh lemon juice

2 cups watercress, torn

2 stalks celery, strings removed, diced

4 ripe yellow or green skinned pears, unpeeled

Extra lemon juice

Honey

Procedure

Toast walnuts in a dry skillet on top of stove over medium heat for about 10 minutes or until slightly brown and fragrant. Remove from pan and let cool.

Whisk together oil and vinegar or lemon juice. You may substitute your favorite dressing as long as it is free of saturated fat and trans fat. Toss watercress, walnuts, and celery with dressing. Core the pears, starting at the top. Slice each pear horizontally in 4 thick slices. Brush cut sides with lemon juice. Place slices, slightly overlapping, on a salad plate. Scatter salad dressing over the pears and drizzle over all with honey.

Serves 4.

Soups

&

Stews

BLACK BEAN SOUP with GARLIC CROUTONS

Beans are high on the list of cholesterol Fighter Foods. Not only do they contain no cholesterol and no saturated fat, but they have been proven in many studies to actually reduce cholesterol. An added benefit here is the olive oil, another Fighter Food. If possible, avoid store bought croutons—they often contain trans fats as well as saturated fats. Always check the label.

Ingredients

2 cups dry black beans
1 ½ quarts cold water
1 teaspoon baking soda
4 tablespoons olive oil
2 large stalks celery, chopped
1 large sweet onion, chopped
1 teaspoon cumin powder
1 teaspoon dried oregano
3 cloves garlic, minced
2 teaspoons fresh lemon juice
Salt and pepper to taste
Lemon slices
½ cup sherry (optional)

Procedure

Soak beans overnight in cold water to cover. Drain. Add beans, 1 ½ cups of water, and baking soda to soup pot. Bring to a full boil. Lower heat and simmer, uncovered, until beans are tender (about 2 hours). Check occasionally during cooking and add more water as needed.

Heat oil in a skillet, and sauté celery and onion with cumin and

cont...

oregano until vegetables are tender crisp. Add garlic, lemon juice, salt, and pepper. Cook until all vegetables are tender. Add to beans and simmer 30 minutes. For a hearty peasant soup, serve as is. For a smoother, more elegant dinner soup, puree in batches in a blender or food processor. Another alternative is to press through a food mill. Return to soup pot, add sherry and salt and pepper, if needed. Reheat slowly. (Alcohol will evaporate with cooking.) Top with garlic croutons and garnish with lemon slices.

Serves 6.

SKILLET GARLIC CROUTONS

Ingredients

7 thick slices of stale bread

2 teaspoons olive oil

1 or 2 cloves garlic, minced

Sea salt and fresh ground black pepper to taste

Procedure

Remove crusts from bread and cut into cubes. Heat olive oil in a skillet over medium low heat and sauté garlic for two or three minutes. Toss in the bread cubes, sprinkle with salt and pepper. Continue to sauté until toasted on all sides.

BLACK BEAN BISQUE

A velvety smooth bisque, elegant enough to be served as a first course for dinner. You may opt to leave this unprocessed and enjoy as a more textured soup. Since this responds well to freezing and is great to have on hand, you may wish to make a double batch.

Ingredients

1 tablespoon extra virgin olive oil

½ cup diced celery

½ cup Vidalia or other sweet onion

½ cup sliced carrots

1 tablespoon minced garlic

1 ½ teaspoons cumin

1 tablespoon fresh chopped oregano or 1 teaspoon dried

¼ teaspoon coarse ground black pepper

2 cups store bought non fat or homemade chicken broth

1 cup cold water

1 tablespoon fresh lemon juice

3 (15 ounce) cans black beans, drained and rinsed in cold water

Procedure

Heat oil in a large soup pot over medium heat. Add celery, onion, and carrots. Cook for 10 minutes or until vegetables are tender. Add garlic, cumin, oregano, and pepper. Cook another 4 minutes. Finally, incorporate the chicken stock, water, lemon juice, and beans. Simmer for 5 minutes.

Process in blender in small batches until smooth. Reheat before serving. Leftovers freeze well.

Serves 8 to 10.

CHICKEN RICE SOUP

Removing the solidified fat is crucial to making this a healthy soup, safe for those who must keep their cholesterol levels down. The rotisserie chicken and store bought chicken broth (stock) save us precious time. Both are rich and tasty, and add to the flavor of this nourishing soup.

Ingredients

1 store bought rotisserie chicken

1 quart cold water

2 (14 ounce) containers organic chicken broth

2 bay leaves

1 sweet onion, chopped

2 stalks celery, chopped

2 large carrots, peeled and sliced

½ teaspoon dried thyme

1 cup rice

Procedure

Skin and bone the chicken, reserving bones and discarding the skin. Set chicken aside to cool, then cover and refrigerate. Meanwhile, place bones in a large soup pot. Add water, broth, and bay leaves. Bring to a boil, reduce heat, and simmer for 2 hours. Allow to cool slightly. Strain through a colander to remove bones and bay leaves. Refrigerate the broth. By the time this is chilled, any fat will have solidified on the surface and is easily removed with a large spoon. Remove chicken from refrigerator and cut into bite size chunks. Add onion, celery, carrots, thyme, rice, and chicken to the pot. Return to boiling. Lower heat and simmer for 20 minutes. Check seasoning and add salt and pepper if desired. Serve with crackers or a good crusty bread.

Serves 4 to 6.

CHICKEN STEW

Here's a put-together-quickly hearty stew that you can make from left-over chicken. Served with a green salad and French bread, it makes for a complete, well balanced, and low cholesterol dinner.

Ingredients

2 tablespoons extra virgin olive oil

2 large carrots, peeled and sliced

2 large celery stalks, peeled and sliced

¼ cup chopped sweet onion

2 cloves garlic, peeled and minced

2 large red potatoes, unpeeled in large chunks

½ teaspoon dried thyme or 1 ½ teaspoons fresh, chopped

2 quarts homemade, or store bought organic chicken stock

1 large bay leaf

¼ cup instant potato flakes

2 cups bite size cut up cooked chicken

Procedure

Warm a large deep heavy skillet over medium high heat. Add the olive oil followed by the carrots, celery, onion, garlic, and potatoes. Cook uncovered until the vegetables are not quite tender, stirring occasionally. Add the chicken stock, thyme, and bay leaf. Simmer for 3 or 4 minutes or until the vegetables are cooked. Remove 1 cup of the hot broth, place in a bowl and whisk in ¼ cup of instant potatoes. Continue to whisk until you have a thick smooth mixture. Briskly stir this into the stew until the broth thickens. Add the cut up chicken and simmer for 1 or 2 minutes more or until chicken is heated through.

Serves 6 to 8.

CHILLED AVOCADO SOUP

Although avocados have a high fat content, studies have shown they actually reduce levels of cholesterol. They also contain 11 vitamins! The lemon juice not only adds flavor but also keeps the avocados from turning brown. Walnuts are high on the list of Fighter Foods (see Chapter 1). This is cool, refreshing, a bit elegant, and sooo good!

Ingredients

4 ripe avocados

2 cups chicken stock

1 tablespoon fresh lemon juice

1 tablespoon fresh tarragon or 1 teaspoon dried

¼ teaspoon Tabasco

½ cup fat free plain yogurt

½ cup fat free sour cream

Crushed toasted walnuts for garnish*

Procedure

Peel avocados and remove the large seed. Heat the chicken stock. Puree the avocado in a blender or food processor and stir into the hot stock. Add lemon juice, tarragon, and Tabasco. Place in refrigerator until thoroughly chilled. Combine the sour cream and yogurt. Stir into the soup and chill again. Serve in small bowls or cups. Garnish with walnuts.

Serves 4.

* To toast the walnuts, place in a dry skillet and cook over medium heat for 5 to 10 minutes.

CHILLED STRAWBERRY SOUP

Cold soups are ideal in hot summer weather or any time a refreshing dish is called for. Serve this as an elegant first course or as a light dessert following a heavy meal. It is low in cholesterol and low in dangerous fats. This makes a colorful presentation and has a fringe benefit: strawberries are high in antioxidants.

Ingredients

1 cup white wine

¼ cup sugar

1 quart cold water

3 tablespoons cornstarch

1 quart strawberries, washed, hulled, and chopped

Fat free mock crème fraîche (see next page)

Procedure

Combine wine, sugar, and water in a soup pot. Bring to a boil. Moisten cornstarch with a little water and stir into the mixture. Boil for 1 minute and allow to cool slightly before adding the strawberries. Chill for several hours. Serve in cold soup bowls (refrigerate them or place in freezer beforehand). Top with mock crème fraîche.

Serves 8-10.

MOCK CRÈME FRAÎCHE
with TOASTED ALMONDS

Ingredients

4 ounces fat free Cool Whip*
4 ounces fat free sour cream
½ cup sliced almonds
Mint leaves

Procedure

Combine the Cool Whip and sour cream. Refrigerate. Spread almonds in a dry skillet and toast over medium heat until golden. Set aside. When you are ready to serve, stir the almonds into the crème fraîche and float a dollop on each bowl of soup. Top off with one or two mint leaves.

Note: Remember to use Cool Whip for special treats only and always in moderation. See Chapter 1: Safe Foods

COLORFUL VEGETARIAN PASTA SOUP

This scrumptious soup includes Parmesan cheese in its ingredients. Beware, even though grated Parmesan cheese is the safest cheese to use, do use it sparingly and only occasionally. All cheeses are high in saturated fat and cholesterol. Some are sold as "low" fat. Read nutrition labels carefully.

cont...

Ingredients

2 tablespoons canola oil

1 cup chopped sweet onion

1 red bell pepper, seeded and chopped

1 yellow bell pepper, seeded and chopped

½ cup sliced mushrooms

1 cup yellow corn kernels

2 cloves garlic, minced

1 (14 ounce) can crushed tomatoes

2 tablespoons fresh chopped basil or ¾ teaspoons dried

1 teaspoon dried oregano

Sea salt and fresh ground black pepper to taste

2 quarts fat free vegetable stock (homemade or store bought)

1 cup uncooked orzo (a pasta that is shaped like rice)

Parmesan Cheese Toast (recipe follows)

Procedure

Heat canola in a soup pot. Add onion and red and yellow peppers. Sauté over medium heat for ten minutes or until vegetables are tender crisp. Stir in mushrooms, corn, garlic, crushed tomatoes, basil, and oregano. Season with salt and pepper. Cook for 2 minutes; stir in the stock. Bring to a boil and add pasta. Follow instructions on package and cook pasta al dente. Ladle into warm soup bowls. Just before serving, float a slice of Parmesan Cheese toast on top. So good!

Serves 8-10.

Jeannie Serpa

PARMESAN CHEESE TOAST

Ingredients

French or any unsliced bread of choice
Extra virgin olive oil
Grated Parmesan cheese
Finely chopped fresh basil

Procedure

Cut bread into one inch thick slices. Brush each slice with olive oil and spread on cookie sheet. Toast under broiler until golden brown, sprinkle lightly with Parmesan cheese and garnish with basil.

COOL as a CUCUMBER SOUP

Place soup bowls in the refrigerator or freezer at least two hours ahead of serving time. Your guests will appreciate this extra touch on a hot summer day.

Ingredients

2 cucumbers
1 tablespoon finely chopped onion
2 cups chicken stock
1 tablespoon chopped fresh dill or 1 teaspoon dried
Salt and white pepper to taste
1 cup fat free plain yogurt
1 cup fat free sour cream
Chopped fresh or dried dill for garnish (optional)

cont...

Procedure

Peel cucumbers, seed, and cut into chunks. Combine onion with chicken broth in a medium size soup pot, bring to a boil, reduce heat, and simmer until the cucumbers are tender (about 5 minutes). Add dill, salt, and pepper. Puree in a blender or food processor. Chill. Combine yogurt and sour cream and stir into the soup. Return to refrigerator until ready to serve. Ladle the cold soup into chilled bowls and garnish with dill.

FRENCH ONION SOUP over BASMATI RICE

For years I made this soup with lots of butter. Now I know better and substitute that butter with olive oil and soft tub margarine. My family thinks it's just as good and I feel confident knowing I'm serving them a hearty soup full of flavor and safe from the ravages of saturated fat. Serve this après ski or on any cold, blustery winter day.

Ingredients

3 large onions
⅓ cup olive oil
¼ cup soft tub margarine
1 ½ quarts store bought, fat free beef broth
1 teaspoon granulated sugar
1 tablespoon soft tub margarine
1 clove garlic, chopped fine
Grated Parmesan cheese
Cayenne pepper

cont...

Procedure

Peel the onions and slice very thin. Separate the rings. In a large deep skillet, heat the oil, add onion rings, and cook very, very slowly over low heat. When onions begin to get transparent, add the ¼ cup margarine and continue cooking over low heat until the onion rings are limp. Meanwhile, pour the beef broth into a separate pot and bring to a boil. Add the boiling broth and sugar to the onions. Raise heat to high and stir gently from the bottom of the pan until the mixture comes to a boil. Add 1 tablespoon margarine and the garlic, reduce heat, and allow to simmer for 15 minutes. Place Basmati rice in the bottom of soup bowls and ladle the soup over the top. (Resist the urge to add the rice and cook it in the soup, it will loose its distinctive nutty flavor.) Sprinkle very lightly with Parmesan cheese and just a dash of cayenne pepper.

Serves 10-12.

BASMATI RICE

Ingredients

2 cups Basmati rice

3 ½ cups cold water

2 teaspoons canola or olive oil

1 teaspoon sea salt

Procedure

Add rice, water, oil, and salt to a saucepan. Bring to a boil, uncovered. Reduce heat, cover, and simmer for 15 minutes. Remove from heat, uncover, stir, and fluff with a fork.

GAZPACHO

Many cold summer soups require cooking before chilling. Here the cook stays cool! Combine these fresh vegetables for an icy, nourishing soup. Fresh vegetables help to lower cholesterol levels. There is no dangerous saturated fat or trans fat in this recipe. The only fat used is the olive oil, which we know helps to reduce cholesterol.

Ingredients

4 ripe tomatoes, peeled and chopped

1 green pepper, chopped

1 cucumber, peeled and chopped

2 stalks celery, chopped

1 small onion, chopped

1 sprig parsley

1 cup dry white wine

1 cup V-8 juice or tomato juice

2 cloves garlic

1 tablespoon fresh lemon juice

1 tablespoon olive oil

½ teaspoon cumin powder

Procedure

Blanche tomatoes by plunging into boiling water for 1 minute. Peel and chop. Mix all ingredients in a large bowl. Puree in small batches in a food processor or blender.

If too thick, thin with more V-8 juice. Chill in refrigerator overnight. To serve, place 2 or 3 ice cubes in the bottom of each bowl before adding soup.

Serves 6.

GEORGIA PEANUT SOUP with CROUTONS

Although peanuts and peanut butter contain saturated fats, studies show that they actually lower cholesterol. A research project conducted by Dr. Penny Kris-Etherton at Penn State concludes that a heart healthy diet should include peanuts. (American Journal of Medicine. December, 1999

Ingredients

3 tablespoons canola oil

1 medium sweet onion, chopped fine

1 tablespoon flour

1 quart chicken stock

¼ cup peanut butter

½ cup fat free half & half cream

1 or 2 dashes Tabasco, according to taste

Procedure

Heat canola oil in a soup pan over medium heat. Add chopped onions and sauté until tender. Sprinkle with flour and stir until well blended. Add chicken stock and heat to simmer, stirring constantly until the mix starts to thicken. Add peanut butter and continue stirring until well combined. Slowly add cream and Tabasco. Heat thoroughly and serve piping hot with toasted croutons.

Serves 4-6.

OVEN TOASTED CROUTONS

Preheat oven to 250°

Ingredients

6 thick slices day old French bread

2 tablespoon olive oil

Salt and pepper to taste

Procedure

Remove crusts from slices of bread, cut into cubes and toss with ¼ cup olive oil, salt, and pepper. Spread on a cookie sheet and bake 10 to 15 minutes or until golden brown. Turn during cooking so that all sides are toasted. If you prefer, you may brown the oiled cubes in a skillet over medium heat. Top each individual bowl of soup with 5 or 6 croutons.

GOLDEN ONION SOUP

My original recipe for Golden Onion Soup from years ago (before I knew better), called for butter, butter, and more butter! This cholesterol safe version tastes just as good. It is rich in flavor and easy to make.

Ingredients

3 large Vidalia or other sweet onions

⅓ cup olive oil

1 ½ quarts fat free store bought or homemade chicken stock

¼ cup soft tub margarine

1 clove garlic, chopped fine

cont...

1 teaspoon granulated sugar

½ cup sherry

French bread

Grated Parmesan cheese

Cayenne pepper

Procedure

Peel onions, thinly slice, then separate the rings. Heat oil in a large, deep pan, add the onions, and cook very slowly over low heat. Meanwhile, bring the stock to a boil in a separate pan.

When onions begin to get transparent, add the margarine and the garlic. Continue cooking over low heat until the rings are limp.

Now gradually add the hot stock and the sugar to the onion rings, stirring from the bottom of the pan until the mixture comes to a boil. Add sherry. Lower the heat and allow to simmer for 15 minutes. Most of the alcohol will evaporate during this final cooking stage.

Slice and toast the bread. Place in the bottom of soup bowls just before serving. Ladle in the soup and sprinkle *lightly* with grated Parmesan and cayenne. You may prefer to float the toast on top, then add the Parmesan and cayenne.

Serves 10-12.

GOOD LUCK LENTIL SOUP

Legend tells us that eating lentils on New Year's Day brings luck throughout the year. I cannot attest to the accuracy of this belief, but I can tell you this is a delectable winter soup that freezes well and is perfect to have on hand for unexpected guests. Serve this piping hot with crusty bread.

Ingredients

1 large sweet onion, chopped

3 carrots, peeled and sliced

2 stalks celery, sliced

1 tablespoon extra virgin olive oil

1 package dried lentils

8 cups cold water

1 can (14 ounce) crushed tomatoes

1 teaspoon oregano

½ teaspoon salt (optional)

½ teaspoon coarse ground black pepper

Procedure

In a large soup pot, sauté onion, carrots, and celery in olive oil until tender crisp. Do not overcook. Add lentils, water, tomatoes, oregano, salt, and pepper. Bring to full boil, lower heat, and simmer gently until the lentils are tender (about 45 minutes). Stir occasionally. Serve with crusty bread.

Yield: 8 to 12 servings.

HEARTY TURKEY VEGETABLE STEW

Plan to freeze leftovers in personal or family size air tight containers. (Handy for last minute low cholesterol meals.)

Ingredients

Leftover meaty turkey carcass

Cold water

3 bay leaves

4 large carrots, peeled and sliced into coins

5 stalks celery, chopped

1 large sweet onion, chopped

1 pound green beans, cut into 1 inch pieces

3 cloves garlic, minced

2 pounds red potatoes, unpeeled, cut into bite size chunks

1 tablespoon chopped fresh thyme or 1 teaspoon powdered thyme

2 tablespoons fresh chopped parsley or 2 teaspoons dried flakes

2 (14 ounce) containers organic turkey or chicken stock

Salt and pepper to taste (optional)

6 or 8 chicken bouillon cubes if needed for flavor

Procedure

Place turkey carcass in a large heavy soup pot. Cover with cold water. Add bay leaves. Bring to a boil, reduce heat, cover, and simmer for at least 3 hours. Allow to cool slightly. Strain through a colander. Be certain all bones are removed. Return turkey and liquid to pot and refrigerate overnight. Do not remove bay leaves.

cont...

The next day skim off all condensed fat that is floating on top of the broth. Bring to a boil, add all the vegetables along with the thyme and parsley. Return to a boil. Reduce heat, cover, and simmer until vegetables are tender. (About 20 minutes.) Finally add the turkey stock. Check seasonings and adjust. If extra richness is desired, stir bouillon cubes into the hot soup until dissolved.

This makes a big pot of soup, easily serving 10 to 12.

HOMEMADE CHICKEN OR TURKEY STOCK

Ingredients

2 leftover cooked chicken carcasses or 1 turkey carcass
Cold water to cover
3 large onions
5 celery stalks
4 medium size carrots
3 cloves garlic
3 bay leaves
1 bunch parsley, leaves only (no stems)
2 sprigs fresh thyme or ½ teaspoon dried
1 teaspoon coarse ground black pepper
1-2 teaspoons sea salt, according to taste

Procedure

Peel and chop onions, celery, and carrots in large chunks. Peel and slice garlic in half. Place carcass, vegetables, bay leaves, parsley, thyme, salt, and pepper in large soup pot. Cover with cold water; bring to a boil. Reduce heat and simmer uncovered for 2 to 2 ½ hours. Stock will reduce and become concentrated. Strain and allow the stock to cool. Refrigerate. Remove congealed fat and freeze in containers until ready to use. Keeps well in freezer for up to 3 months.

NOT YOUR ORDINARY TURKEY SOUP

This quick and easy soup tastes like you've labored hours over a hot stove. The chicken stock combined with the pan juices from the tomatoes forms a rich flavorful broth, resulting in a thick, nutritious, and cholesterol friendly soup. If using deli turkey for this recipe, be certain that it's free of saturated fat.

Ingredients

1 quart box store bought chicken stock (broth)

2 carrots, peeled and sliced

2 celery stalks, strings removed and sliced

1 clove garlic, peeled and minced

¼ cup rice

¼ teaspoon dried thyme

1 bay leaf

2 vine ripened tomatoes

1 tablespoon extra virgin olive oil

½ teaspoon dried onion flakes or 1 tablespoon minced onion

¼ teaspoon dried sweet basil

⅛ teaspoon oregano

Sea salt

1 cup cut up leftover or deli turkey

Procedure

In a medium size saucepan, bring chicken stock to boil. Add carrots, celery, garlic, and rice. Reduce heat, add thyme and bay leaf. Simmer, covered, for 15 minutes. Meanwhile, cut tomatoes into large chunks. Heat olive oil in a skillet over medium high heat. Add tomatoes, onion, basil, and oregano. Sprinkle with salt to taste. Reduce heat, cover and simmer for 5-10 minutes or until

cont...

tomatoes are tender but still intact. Add the cooked tomato mixture along with the cut up turkey to the saucepan containing the broth and rice. Cook over medium heat 2-3 minutes, allowing the flavors to blend.

Serves 4.

QUICK AND THICK COMFORT CHICKEN STEW

Nourishing, hot, and oh so good! You don't need to be ill to enjoy this stew. Perfect following a hockey game, après ski or sledding.

Ingredients

2 quarts chicken broth, store bought or homemade

4 cut up unpeeled red potatoes

3 peeled and thick sliced carrots

2 teaspoons minced sweet onion or 1 teaspoon dried onion flakes

2 cloves garlic, peeled and sliced

1 teaspoon chopped fresh thyme or ⅓ teaspoon dried

3 teaspoons fresh chopped parsley or 1 teaspoon dried

2 teaspoons fresh lemon juice

1 cup bite size pieces of cooked chicken

Sea salt and black pepper

cont...

Procedure

Place broth, potatoes, and carrots in a soup pot. Bring to a boil, reduce heat, cover, and simmer until vegetables are soft. With a potato masher, mash the potatoes and carrots while they are still in the broth. Return to heat and bring once again to a boil. Add onion, garlic, thyme, parsley, and lemon juice. Reduce heat, and let bubble uncovered until broth thickens (5-10 minutes). Add salt and pepper to taste. Add chicken, cook 2 minutes until chicken is hot. This is even better served on the second day. Great with crusty French bread.

Serves 4-6.

RICH, PEPPERY CHICKEN SOUP
over TEXMATI RICE

My very favorite quick to cook chicken soup. The secret is to serve the soup over the rice. Texmati rice does not respond well to being cooked in soup. Cooking it separately from the soup preserves its nutty flavor. "If you should go overboard with the red pepper, be sure to have good crusty bread at the ready! Bread, not water, will do more to put out the fire."

Ingredients

2 cups Texmati Rice

3 ½ cups cold water

2 teaspoons canola oil

1 teaspoon sea salt

3 quarts store bought or homemade chicken broth

2 cups cut up cooked chicken

3 large carrots, peeled and sliced thick

3 celery stalks, sliced thick

cont...

¼ of a large Vidalia or other sweet onion, chopped

3 cloves garlic, chopped

1 teaspoon or more dried red pepper flakes, according to taste

1 large or 2 small bay leaves.

½ teaspoon dried or 1 ½ teaspoon fresh chopped thyme

Celery salt

Cook the rice

Combine rice, water, oil, and salt in a saucepan. Bring to a boil, reduce heat and simmer, covered, for exactly 15 minutes. Uncover and fluff with a fork.

Procedure

Pour the chicken broth into a large soup pot. Bring to a boil and add chicken, carrots, celery, onion, garlic, and red pepper flakes. For a slight peppery flavor, adhere to the ½ teaspoon. If you like your food with a good deal of heat, go with the full teaspoon or more. Keep in mind, however, that the peppery flavor increases with cooking! Reduce heat, cover, and simmer gently for 10 to 15 minutes or until vegetables are tender. Do not add the rice to the soup!!

To serve, spoon about ½ to ¾ cup of rice into each soup bowl. Sprinkle very lightly with celery salt. Ladle soup over the rice. Present while piping hot with hot pepper sauce on the side for the brave of heart!

Serves 10-12.

TURKEY GOULASH

Hungarian Goulash is traditionally a thick stew made with beef, vegetables and paprika, all cooked with butter. Here is a friendly version of goulash that is low in cholesterol and saturated fat, yet fully as delicious as the real thing. Paprika is important to this dish since it lends both flavor and color.

Ingredients

½ pound elbow macaroni

2 tablespoons olive oil

1 pound lean ground turkey breast

1 red bell pepper, seeded and chopped

3 stalks celery, chopped

1 sweet onion, peeled and chopped

1 tablespoon sweet paprika

1 teaspoon cumin

½ teaspoon oregano

1 clove garlic, minced

¼ to ½ teaspoon freshly ground black pepper, according to taste

1 cup chicken broth, homemade or organic store bought

1 cup fat free sour cream

Chopped fresh parsley for garnish

Procedure

Bring a pot of salted water to a boil for the macaroni. Meanwhile, warm olive oil in a large deep skillet over medium high heat. Add the ground turkey, breaking up and crumbling with a spoon. Cook until no longer pink (about 4 minutes) then stir in red pepper, celery, and onion along with paprika, cumin,

cont...

oregano, and garlic. Continue cooking until vegetables are tender crisp (about 5 minutes), then add the black pepper.

Remove from heat. Leave chicken and vegetables in the skillet.

By now the water is boiling and ready for the pasta. Cook al dente according to package directions, roughly 6 minutes.

Add the chicken broth and sour cream to the skillet, bring to a bubble, reduce heat, and simmer the mixture an additional 5 minutes. Incorporate the drained macaroni and continue to simmer an additional minute or two. If the goulash is too thick, just add a little more broth. Since the pasta is cooked in salted water and the sour cream has great flavor, additional salt should not be needed. Nevertheless, taste test and adjust if necessary. Garnish with parsley.

Yields 4 generous servings.

VEGETARIAN BEAN SOUP

Many varieties of beans (kidney, cranberry, pinto, white, navy, black, and others) are available cooked and canned, ready to be used in soups and salads. Be sure to drain them before adding to soups. Drain and rinse in cold water before adding to salads. Do not confuse these with canned baked beans like Campbell's or Bush's.

Ingredients

2 tablespoons olive oil

2 stalks celery, chopped

2 onions, chopped

3 cloves garlic, minced

2 ½ quarts cold water or chicken stock

1 pound fresh green beans, cut into 1 inch pieces

cont...

1 carrot, peeled and sliced into coins

3 tomatoes, blanched, peeled, and cut into large chunks

1 ½ tablespoons chopped fresh basil or ½ teaspoon dried

4 cups canned kidney beans, drained

Chopped parsley (optional)

Salt and fresh ground black pepper to taste

Procedure

Heat oil in a soup pot. Add celery and onions and sauté until tender crisp. Add garlic and cook another 3 minutes. Blanch tomatoes by plunging them in boiling water for 1 minute, making them easy to peel. Add water, green beans, carrot, tomatoes, and basil. Bring to a boil, reduce heat, and simmer until vegetables are tender. Add more water if necessary. Stir in the kidney beans and cook 10 minutes or until hot, but not boiling. Add salt and black pepper.

Yields 8-10 servings.

Main Dishes

EGGS AND CEREAL

CRABMEAT OMELET

Serve this scrumptious breakfast treat with Lemon Blueberry or Pineapple Pecan Muffins. Recipes for both can be found in the Bread and Rolls section of this book. The muffins can be made ahead and stored in the refrigerator or freezer. Warm them briefly in your microwave oven before serving.

Ingredients

4 green onions (scallions)

1 tablespoon canola oil

12 ounces egg substitute

½ cup skim milk

¾ teaspoon sea salt

⅛ teaspoon freshly ground black pepper

⅛ teaspoon paprika

6 ounces fresh or imitation crabmeat

Procedure

If you are using fresh crabmeat, drain and flake with a fork. For imitation crab, chop small. Set aside.

Slice the onions, including the tops, very thin. Use a large non-stick skillet, add canola, and sauté onions over medium heat for 2 or 3 minutes. Meanwhile, beat egg substitute slightly with a fork and add milk, salt, pepper, and paprika. Pour the egg mixture over the onion and cook slowly until firm and golden brown on the bottom. When done, scatter the crabmeat over the omelet, fold, and turn out on a hot platter.

Serves 4.

HOT CEREAL SUPREME

Those store bought individual packets of flavored oatmeal may seem convenient (just add water and microwave), but they are high in sodium and sugar. This do-it-yourself recipe allows you to control the amount of salt, sugar, and spices. The raisins supply natural sweetness and you may find the optional brown sugar unnecessary. Vary the amounts of fruit according to taste. Try different combinations such as dried sweet cranberries and chopped walnuts or simply cut up fresh peaches. Each ½ cup serving of oatmeal yields 2 grams of soluble fiber. For more information see chapter #2.

Ingredients

½ cup oatmeal

1 tablespoon chopped apples

1 tablespoon golden raisins

½ teaspoon cinnamon

Dash salt

1 ¼ cups cold water

1 tablespoon fat free half & half cream

Brown sugar (optional)

Procedure

Combine cereal, apples, raisins, cinnamon, salt, and water in a microwavable bowl. Microwave on high for 2 minutes. Remove and stir. Add half & half and sprinkle lightly with brown sugar if desired. Be sure to use a bowl that's deep enough to allow for overflow. Oatmeal will "bubble up" during cooking.

Serves one.

POPCORN for BREAKFAST? WHY NOT?

Kids will think this is oh, so funny and feel they're getting to eat a snack for breakfast. I happen to know an adult who loves this also! Popcorn is nutritious with zero cholesterol, and free of both saturated fat and trans fat. Blueberries and raisins are high in antioxidants. This is fun and so much better than store brought cereals that are full of sugar and salt.

Ingredients

Natural popcorn, lightly salted

Brown sugar

Skim milk or fat free half & half cream

Blueberries or raisins

Procedure

Pour popcorn into a cereal bowl. Sprinkle with a small amount of brown sugar. Add 1 or 2 tablespoons of milk or cream and top with berries or raisins.

"A good meal makes a man feel more charitable toward the whole world than any sermon."

—Arthur Pendenys

SAVORY SCRAMBLED EGG WHITES

Think you could not possibly tolerate scrambled egg whites? These are truly savory, with lots of flavor and a tad of zip. Here you have no saturated fat and no cholesterol. Remember, cholesterol lurks in the yolks of eggs. Two whole eggs, extra large, can net you 500 grams of cholesterol, 300 grams more than the recommended daily amount.

Ingredients

6 egg whites

2 heaping teaspoons fat free plain yogurt

¾ teaspoon Dijon mustard

2 teaspoons finely chopped chives or 1 teaspoon dried onion flakes

Coarse ground black pepper to taste

Canola cooking spray

Paprika (optional)

Procedure

Use a fork to whip together the egg whites, yogurt, and mustard until well combined. Stir in the chives and pepper. Heat a skillet over medium heat, remove from stove, hold over the sink, and spray generously with canola. (This extra step will save you cleanup time since the spray will mess up your stove top, or worse, cause a flare up!) Return to stove and add the egg mixture. Scramble with a fork, cooking quickly. When eggs are light and fluffy, remove from heat. Do not overcook. Dust lightly with paprika for color and additional flavor. Great with muffins and a side of fruit.

Serves 2.

SCRAMBLED EGGS and TOASTED MUFFINS

For years my idea of scrambled eggs involved cream and lots of butter. A total cholesterol count of 314 led to the development of this book and I now enjoy my eggs cooked as shown here. Prepared in this manner, I actually prefer the whites over the egg substitute. Most food preferences are based on habit. Break that habit and try these.

Ingredients

3 egg whites or 4 ounces egg substitute

1 tablespoon fat free sour cream

½ teaspoon chopped chives (fresh or freeze dried)

Coarse ground pepper

Kosher salt

Canola oil cooking spray

2 Pumpkin Pie Muffins*

Fat free or reduced fat lemon yogurt

Sliced oranges and strawberries

Procedure

For each serving, whip eggs and sour cream together with a fork. Stir in the chives.

Heat a heavy skillet over medium heat, spray with canola, add egg mixture, season with salt and pepper. Cook quickly, stirring constantly. Transfer to a warm plate. Cut a Pumpkin Pie muffin in half horizontally and toast in toaster oven or under broiler. Spread with lemon yogurt. Serve with a side of sliced oranges and strawberries.

> * Note: Look in the BREADS and MUFFINS section for Pumpkin Pie Muffin recipe.

SMOKED SALMON SCRAMBLED EGGS

An elegant breakfast or brunch, this dish has it all. The eggs are cholesterol friendly with the additional benefits of salmon and olive oil, both proven to help lower cholesterol. Add the muffins with their cholesterol lowering oat bran and nuts, then the fresh fruit and you are doing everything right! And the taste? Out of this world!

Ingredients

¼ cup fat free sour cream

1 teaspoon minced shallots

9 extra large egg whites or 12 ounces egg substitute

3 tablespoons fat free half & half cream

2 teaspoons chopped chives, divided

Sea Salt to taste

1 tablespoon canola oil

4 ounces smoked salmon, chopped

Coarse ground black pepper to taste

Procedure

Mix together sour cream and shallots. Set aside. Whisk together eggs, cream, one teaspoon of the chives, and salt. Heat oil in a skillet over medium heat. Add egg mixture and cook slightly, stirring constantly. Add smoked salmon. Continue cooking no more than a minute or until eggs are cooked but still moist. Remove from heat immediately and place a dollop of the sour cream mixture on each serving of eggs. Sprinkle with pepper and remaining chives. Serve with Pineapple Pecan Muffins and fresh fruit.

Serves 3 or 4.

Note: See recipe for Pineapple and Pecan Muffins under BREADS and ROLLS.

WHITE FRITTATA

"Whoever heard of a white frittata?" you ask. Well I hadn't either until I invented this one. Trust me, you will enjoy this colorful, savory dish. No egg yolks, therefore no cholesterol!

Ingredients

1 tablespoon canola oil

1 tablespoon chopped onion

¼ cup diced green pepper

Salt and pepper to taste

1 teaspoon chopped fresh basil or ⅓ teaspoon dried

¼ cup chopped tomato

3 egg whites

1 tablespoon water

Procedure

Warm canola in a nonstick skillet over medium heat. Add onion, green pepper, basil, salt, and pepper. Sauté until vegetables are tender crisp. Next stir in tomatoes, cooking just until tomatoes are hot. (They need to be firm.) Combine water and egg whites. Use a fork to whip to a slightly frothy stage.

Carefully pour eggs over the vegetables. Cover and cook over low heat until all this starts to set. As soon as cooking is complete, loosen the edges of your frittata with a plastic spatula, then slide onto a warm plate.

Single serving.

MEATS

HAM STEAK with MUSTARD SAUCE

Once I had my cholesterol under control, I found I could indulge in an occasional serving of low fat ham. Always grill or broil ham steaks, rather than pan fry, allowing any remaining fat to drain off. This delicious mustard sauce has just the right amount of piquancy to make it the perfect accompaniment to ham's sweet-salty flavor. I use this cholesterol friendly recipe both as a thick sauce for ham and as a dip for raw vegetables.

Ingredients

⅔ cup fat free sour cream

⅔ cup fat free plain yogurt

¼ cup Dijon mustard

2 tablespoons fresh dill, chopped or 2 teaspoon dried

2 (1 pound) extra lean ham steaks

Procedure

Whisk together first four ingredients. Place in the refrigerator for 20 minutes, allowing the flavors to blend before serving.

Meanwhile, trim any visible fat from the steaks and grill over medium high heat or broil on a rack 3 or 4 inches from heat, turning half way through cooking. Place cooked ham on a platter and pour over some of the sauce. Serve remaining sauce in a gravy boat on the side. Makes about 1 ½ cups.

Recipe serves 4-5.

PORK ROAST with SWEET & SOUR SAUCE

If you are at a point in your cholesterol journey where you are allowed an occasional serving of very lean, fat trimmed pork, choose a loin pork roast and cook it with this excellent sauce.

Preheat oven to 325°

Ingredients

5 pound roast loin of pork

1 teaspoon dried sage

1 teaspoon sea salt

1 teaspoon coarse ground black pepper

1 (8 ounce) can crushed pineapple, with juice

⅓ cup sugar

½ cup apple cider vinegar

1 tablespoon soy sauce

1 tablespoon cornstarch mixed with 1 tablespoon cold water

⅔ cup plum jam

Procedure

Trim any visible fat from the roast. Combine sage, salt, and pepper in a small bowl. Rub the pork well with mixture. Insert a meat thermometer into the center of the meat. Place on a rack in a roasting pan and roast, allowing about 25 minutes per pound.

Meanwhile, make the sauce. Combine pineapple, sugar, vinegar, soy sauce, and cornstarch mixture in a saucepan. Over medium heat cook to a boiling point, stirring constantly until thick. Lastly, stir in the plum jam. Allow to cool. Makes 2 cups.

After roasting the pork 1 ½ hours, remove from oven and pour

cont...

off excess melted fat. Baste the roast with the sauce and return to oven for 1 hour or until the internal temperature registers 160-165°. Baste again during this last hour. Remove from oven, place on a serving platter and let it stand for 15 minutes before carving. Slice and serve remaining sauce on the side.

STEAK with GRILLING SAUCE

Important! Once you have your cholesterol count under control and are at the point where you can have an occasional serving of lean beef, treat yourself to a good grilled tenderloin steak. When buying beef, choose the leanest cuts. Look for the word "round" or 'loin' in the name. For example: top round, ground round, or tenderloin. Always trim all visible fat, and to be absolutely sure, grill or broil your meat rather than pan fry so that any remaining fat will drain off.

Ingredients

½ cup ketchup

2 tablespoons molasses

2 tablespoons Balsamic vinegar

4 tenderloin steaks

Procedure

In a small bowl, whisk together ketchup, molasses, and vinegar. Brush the steaks with this savory sauce before and during grilling.

Makes ¾ cup.

PASTA

BAKED PASTA with FRESH CHUNKY TOMATO SAUCE

A delightful fresh alternative to the long cooking tomato sauces. The vegetables here are chunky and still crisp. The red pepper adds heat. Eliminate it for a mild sauce or increase it if you like your sauce hot. Tube pastas like ziti or rigatoni work well with this sauce as opposed to the more delicate pastas. Cholesterol and vegetarian friendly!

Preheat oven to 350°

Ingredients

3 tablespoons extra virgin olive oil

3 carrots, diced

3 stalks celery, chopped

2 shallots, chopped

1 clove garlic, minced

4 large red ripe tomatoes, cut in wedges

Kosher salt

Black coarse ground pepper

3-4 dashes dried red pepper flakes

½ teaspoon dried or 1 ½ tablespoons fresh basil

¼ teaspoon dried or ¾ tablespoon fresh oregano

1 (14 ounce) package ziti

1 tablespoon extra virgin olive oil

1 teaspoon salt

cont...

Procedure

Sauté carrots, celery, and shallots in olive oil until slightly tender but crisp. Add garlic, tomatoes, salt and pepper to taste, basil, oregano, and red pepper. Cover and simmer until tomato wedges are barely soft and still intact. Sauce should be slightly "juicy." Add olive oil if needed. Meanwhile, cook ziti according to package directions, adding olive oil and salt to the water. Drain the pasta and place in a casserole dish. Stir in tomato sauce and bake for 15 - 20 minutes, allowing flavors to marry. A green salad and crusty Italian bread are excellent accompaniments.

Serves 4.

LIGHT and LIVELY ANGEL HAIR PASTA
with GARLIC BREAD

Serve this refreshing pasta dish with a green salad and baked garlic bread. Parmesan cheese is the safest cheese to use when following a low cholesterol program. Always use SPARINGLY and only occasionally. An added benefit here is the extra virgin olive oil, known to reduce cholesterol.

Ingredients

1 teaspoon olive oil

1 teaspoon sea salt

8 ounce package Angel Hair pasta

⅓ cup extra virgin olive oil

2 cloves garlic, minced

1 ¼ cups fresh parsley or 1 tablespoon dried

1 ½ teaspoons fresh chopped oregano or ½ teaspoon dried

cont...

1 teaspoon coarse ground black pepper

2 tablespoons freshly squeezed lemon juice

1 tablespoon Parmesan cheese

Extra virgin olive oil

Extra lemon juice

Procedure

Bring a pot of water to a rolling boil, add olive oil, salt, and pasta, cook according to package directions and drain. Set aside. Add ⅓ cup olive oil and garlic to a large skillet. Cook over medium heat, stirring constantly until the garlic is slightly transparent. Stir in the cooked Angel Hair, parsley, oregano, pepper, and lemon juice. Heat until warmed through. Add more olive oil if needed. For more piquancy, you may wish to add extra lemon juice. Sprinkle lightly with the Parmesan and serve immediately.

Makes two generous portions.

GARLIC BREAD

Preheat oven to 375°

Ingredients

1 loaf unsliced Italian bread

Olive Oil

Garlic salt

Fresh ground black pepper

cont...

Procedure

Slice the loaf of bread horizontally, being careful not to cut all the way through. Whisk together oil, garlic salt, and pepper. Brush the inside of loaf liberally with the olive oil mixture. Wrap entire loaf in aluminum foil and bake 10 to 15 minutes or until piping hot. Serve, cut into 1 inch slices.

LINGUINE with CILANTRO SAUCE

Here's a variation of pesto sauce, made with cilantro in place of basil, hazelnuts in place of pine nuts, and no cheese. Perfect for those who are trying to lower cholesterol, this dish has a smooth, refreshing flavor. If you simply must have cheese, sprinkle with just a little grated parmesan. Hazelnuts are high on my list of cholesterol lowering foods.

Preheat oven to 350°

Ingredients

⅓ cup hazelnuts

1 bunch fresh cilantro

1 package (usually 12 ounces) linguine

1 teaspoon extra virgin olive oil

1 teaspoon salt

6 tablespoon extra virgin olive oil

3 cloves garlic

1 teaspoon salt (or substitute 1 tablespoon fresh lemon juice)

Procedure

Place hazelnuts on a dry cookie sheet and toast in oven for 10 to 15 minutes. Most of the skin can then be removed by rubbing

cont...

with a clean dish towel. While the nuts are toasting, wash cilantro in cold water. Drain.

Meanwhile, cook the pasta with 1 teaspoon olive oil and salt according to package instructions. While the pasta is cooking, chop the toasted hazelnuts. Place the nuts with the cilantro, 5 tablespoons of the olive oil, garlic, and salt in a blender or food processor. Pulse 3 or 4 times and blend just enough to make a smooth sauce. Warm the remaining tablespoonful of extra olive oil in a saucepan, then add the sauce. Cook on low until heated through. (About 1 minute.)

When linguine is cooked, drain, return to pot, add sauce, toss lightly, and serve immediately. Scrumptious!

Serves 4.

"Herbs do comfort the wearied brain with fragrant smells which yield a certain kind of nourishment."

—William Coles

POULTRY

APRICOT SWEET and SOUR CHICKEN
over JASMINE RICE

This is an excellent company dish. Your guests will never know, unless you tell them, that this savory dish is helping to lower their cholesterol! Though this recipe may appear at first glance to be long and complicated, it goes together quickly.

Preheat oven to 400°

Ingredients

1 teaspoon Dijon mustard

1 clove garlic, minced

½ jar apricot jam (about 5 ounces)

1 tablespoon brown sugar

¼ cup white wine vinegar

¼ cup low sodium soy sauce

½ cup ketchup

¼ cup chopped scallions (green onions)

¼ cup chopped fresh parsley

4 chicken breast halves, boned and skinned with fat removed

Coarse sea salt

Freshly ground pepper

Canola cooking spray

½ cup seasoned breadcrumbs

1 cup Jasmine rice

1 ¾ cups cold water

½ teaspoon sea salt

1 teaspoon canola oil

cont...

Procedure

Thoroughly combine mustard, garlic, jam, sugar, vinegar, soy sauce, ketchup, scallions, and parsley in a medium size bowl. Set this sauce aside, allowing the flavors to marry.

Place chicken breast halves between two sheets of plastic wrap and flatten with the bottom of a small heavy skillet or a wooden kitchen mallet. Sprinkle both sides lightly with salt and pepper. Generously coat a baking dish with canola spray. Place bread-crumbs in a separate flat dish and press chicken into the crumbs to coat. Position the breaded chicken in the baking dish. Bake for 10 minutes. Remove from oven. Spoon the apricot sauce on and around the chicken. Reduce oven heat to 325°. Continue baking for another 15 minutes or until juices run clear when the center of breast halves are pierced with a fork. Test carefully. If juices are still pink, return to oven for 5 minutes and test again.

While chicken is baking, cook the Jasmine rice: Place rice in a saucepan with water, salt, and canola oil. Bring to a boil, reduce heat to simmer and cook, covered, for 15 minutes or until water is absorbed. Remove from heat, fluff with a fork, and leave uncovered for 3 or 4 minutes. Spread the rice on a warm platter, top with chicken, and spoon the apricot sauce on and around all.

Makes 4 servings.

CHICKEN a l'ORANGE #1

You may love Duck a l'Orange, but since duck is extremely high in saturated fat, it is one of the more harmful dishes for those of us who must watch cholesterol levels. Here is my safe and savory answer. It's much simpler to make than an authentic Duck a l'Orange but every bit as delicious. For Chicken Stock recipe look in the Soup Section.

Ingredients

2 chicken breast halves, skinless but with bone

1 tablespoon olive oil

Sea salt

Black freshly ground pepper

1 cup organic chicken broth from carton (or homemade chicken stock)

1 bay leaf

½ cup orange marmalade

1 tablespoon store bought raspberry vinaigrette, free of saturated fat

1 tablespoon fresh lemon juice

1 tablespoon Grand Marnier (optional)

Procedure

Heat olive oil in a deep heavy skillet over medium high heat. Sprinkle both sides of chicken with salt and pepper. Sear both sides of breasts until lightly browned (about 1-2 minutes each side). Add chicken broth and bay leaf, cover and simmer for roughly 15 minutes or until breasts are still pink in the center. Turn chicken half way through cooking.

Meanwhile, in a small bowl combine orange marmalade, raspberry vinaigrette, lemon juice, and Grand Marnier.

cont...

Uncover the skillet, remove chicken and set aside. Turn up heat and allow the broth to bubble and reduce by one half. Stir in marmalade mixture.

Return breasts to the skillet. Continue cooking, uncovered, until the orange sauce has thickened and the chicken is no longer pink inside. This takes only about five minutes.

Plate the chicken and pour over about half the sauce.

Serve remaining sauce on the side.

Serves 2.

CHICKEN a l'ORANGE #2

The traditional Duck a l'Orange is a complicated recipe that starts out with a thick brown sauce made with beef stock. My Chicken a l'Orange #2 is a cholesterol safe, simplified recipe with all the shortcuts I could muster to make this recipe quick and easy.

ORANGE SAUCE (Make this first.)

Ingredients

1 package Knorr's Roasted Turkey Gravy Mix

1 ¼ cups cold water

½ cup orange marmalade

1 tablespoon fresh lemon juice

1 teaspoon white vinegar

1 teaspoon dried onion flakes or 1 tablespoon minced sweet onion

⅛ teaspoon coarse ground black pepper

cont...

Procedure

In a small saucepan, whisk together the turkey gravy mix and water. Bring to a boil over high heat, stirring constantly. Reduce heat and simmer, uncovered for 5 minutes, stirring occasionally or until thick. Whisk in marmalade, lemon juice, vinegar, onion, and black pepper. Continue to simmer for 10 minutes, stirring occasionally. Remove from heat and let cool slightly while you "ready" the chicken.

COMPLETING the DISH

Preheat oven to 325°

Ingredients

   3 boneless, skinless chicken breast halves
   Sea salt
   Coarse ground black pepper

Procedure

Lightly sprinkle both sides of breast halves with salt and pepper. Place in a medium size roasting pan or a foil roasting pan, approximately 9"x 11"x 2". Pour the sauce over the chicken and roast for 20 minutes or until chicken is no longer pink in the center. Half way through the roasting, baste chicken with sauce in pan. Pour any extra sauce in a small bowl to present on the side.

Serves 3. Recipe may be doubled to serve 6.

CHICKEN FARMER'S PIE

This is my take on Shepherd's Pie, traditionally made in England with lamb, in America with ground beef. We need to avoid fatty beef and lamb in order to keep that cholesterol under control. Friends and family will love this savory one dish meal. Can be made ahead and refrigerated, in which case, increase baking time by 10-15 minutes.

Ingredients

2 rotisserie chickens fresh from the deli (If you prefer, roast your own 4 pound chicken)

5 Idaho or Russet potatoes

Cold water

Salt and pepper as you wish

3 tablespoons soft tub margarine

½ cup skim milk

1 cup fat free half & half cream

3 tablespoons dried or fresh chopped chives

1 pound fresh green beans

1 cup chopped celery

1 cup carrots sliced in coins

2 tablespoons canola oil

⅓ cup cold water

½ cup fat free organic chicken broth, store bought or homemade

Paprika

Canola cooking spray

cont...

Procedure

Skin and bone the chicken while it's still warm (much easier). Set aside in a bowl and cover loosely with foil. Pour off any juice that remains in the rotisserie container or roasting pan. Refrigerate until fat solidifies on top (at least an hour). This is saturated fat, the "bad" fat that we must avoid. Skim it off and discard. The remaining good juice will have jelled. Set this aside; it is rich and full of flavor.

Meanwhile, peel potatoes, cut into large chunks, and place in a large pot. Cover with cold water, add salt to taste, bring to a boil over high heat, then lower heat and simmer for 15 minutes or until the potatoes are tender. Drain, add margarine and skim milk. Beat with electric mixer on low setting until smooth, then add half & half. Continue beating on high until soft and creamy, adding more half & half if needed. Stir in chives.

At this point, set oven to 350°.

Place green beans, celery, and carrots in a microwaveable bowl, add canola oil plus ⅓ cup of cold water, salt, and pepper to taste. Microwave on high for 7 minutes or until vegetables are crispy tender. Drain and set aside.

Place the chicken "jell" in a covered bowl in microwave. Warm on high for about one minute. The jell will liquefy. Cut chicken into bite size chunks and spread in bottom of 9x13 inch baking dish. Pour the liquefied jell mixture over the chicken, then the chicken stock. Layer the cooked vegetables on the top then slather on those creamy whipped potatoes, spreading them evenly.

Mist the potato layer with canola baking spray and sprinkle generously with paprika. If your cholesterol level is under control, live a little and dot the potato surface with soft tub margarine instead of misting with canola. Do add the paprika though. It adds flavor and color. Place on middle rack in oven and bake 30 minutes or until heated through. This is a meal in itself. Present it with a simple green salad.

Serves 6-8.

CRISPY BAKED CHICKEN WITH GARLICKY SPINACH

About Garlic

Though the jury is still out when it comes to the merits of garlic's ability to lower cholesterol, you will see it here and in many of my recipes. It certainly adds flavor and nutrition to many dishes. Studies that had previously shown garlic to be good for our cholesterol are being disputed. It seems we would need to consume 12 to 15 cloves a day (at least) in order to produce a slight lowering effect and even that is being contested. As to garlic supplements, according to the Agency for Healthcare Research and Quality (part of the U.S. Department of Health and Human Services), none of the typical claims like "Clinically proven to lower cholesterol" are backed by good scientific evidence. Until we learn otherwise, let's simply enjoy garlic for its flavor and possible nutritional value.

Preheat oven to 400°

Ingredients

3 ½ pounds chicken cut up, skin removed

3 tablespoons Dijon mustard

2 cups multigrain cereal flakes, crushed

2 tablespoons olive oil

Kosher salt

Fresh ground black pepper

Canola cooking spray

1 package (14 ounces) prewashed baby spinach

2 cloves garlic, sliced thin

2 tablespoons toasted pine nuts

cont...

Procedure

In a large bowl, toss the chicken with the mustard to coat. Set aside.

In a separate bowl, mix cereal flakes, 1 tablespoon of the oil, and ¼ teaspoon each salt and pepper. Coat the chicken pieces with the cereal flakes mixture. Lightly coat a cookie sheet with canola cooking spray. Arrange chicken on the sheet and bake until golden and cooked through (45 to 50 minutes) or until juices run clear when chicken is pierced with a fork.

Meanwhile, heat remaining olive oil in a large deep skillet over medium heat. Add the garlic and spinach. Sprinkle with salt and pepper. Toss with tongs while cooking until wilted only, 2 minutes or so. Remove from heat, scatter pine nuts over the top, and serve with chicken.

GRILLED ROSEMARY CHICKEN

Since preparations for this are done in advance, this saves time when coming to the actual cooking. Due to the ingredients in the marinade, the flavor here is extraordinary. It is of prime importance that you remove the skin before serving. Although it is tempting to eat the skin, remember: this is where the dangerous fats reside!

Ingredients

3 large cloves garlic, minced

3 tablespoons extra virgin olive oil

3 tablespoons Dijon mustard

2 tablespoons fresh lemon juice

cont...

2 teaspoons dried rosemary leaves

1 teaspoon coarse ground pepper

3 ½ pounds chicken breasts with skin and bone, halved

Procedure

Whisk together garlic, oil, mustard, and lemon juice until creamy in texture. Add rosemary and pepper. Place chicken in a casserole or glass baking dish. Brush each piece on both sides with the mixture. Cover. Refrigerate overnight or for at least 6 hours.

To grill outdoors

Bring grill to medium heat. Position chicken on grill with skin side down. Cook about 12 minutes, then turn. Continue grilling 20-25 minutes more or until chicken is no longer pink inside. Before serving, remove skin.

To broil indoors:

Preheat broiler. Place chicken in a broiling pan skin side down, 7 to 9 inches from heat. Cook about 25 minutes, then turn and continue broiling 20 minutes or until chicken is no longer pink inside. Remove skin before serving.

Serves 4 to 6.

HONEY LIME CHICKEN BREASTS

A mouth watering entrée with a thick flavorful sauce that clings to the chicken. This makes lowering your cholesterol pure joy! Skinning the chicken before cooking removes the saturated fat (bad) fat. Serve this with mashed potatoes and tender crisp broccoli or green beans and cranberry sauce for color and flavor contrast.

Preheat oven to 350°

Ingredients

4 boned and skinned chicken breasts

1 tablespoon honey

1 tablespoon olive oil

1 clove garlic, minced

1 teaspoon dried or 1 tablespoon fresh chopped thyme

Zest (grated rind) and juice of 1 lime

Fresh ground black pepper

Procedure

Place chicken breasts in a shallow baking pan. In a small bowl, whisk together honey, oil, garlic, thyme, lime zest, and juice. Spoon mixture over the breasts and sprinkle with pepper. Bake 35-40 minutes, basting every 10 minutes. Cook until juices run clear when the chicken is pierced with a folk or skewer. If juices are pink, return to oven and continue cooking for 5 minutes then test again. The liquid in the pan will thicken into a sauce as the chickens cooks.

Serves 4.

LEMON CHICKEN SALAD

Light, refreshing, and different, this salad will have your guests asking for the recipe. Marinating the chicken before grilling adds another dimension to its flavor. This, along with the sweet-tart lemon dressing, results in an intriguing gourmet delight.

Ingredients

4 chicken breasts halves, about 4 oz. each, boneless with skin removed

½ cup fat free bottled sesame ginger marinade

¼ cup slivered almonds

½ cup mandarin oranges

2 stalks celery, chopped

1 cup fat free lemon yogurt

1 tablespoon fresh lemon juice

Mesculin salad greens

Additional mandarin oranges for garnish

Procedure

Pour marinade over chicken and allow to sit in refrigerator for 15 minutes. Wrap chicken in foil and grill for 10-15 minutes or until thoroughly cooked. (Chicken is cooked if juices run clear, not pink, when chicken is pierced with a fork.) Unwrap the chicken, cool, and cut into bite-size pieces. Meanwhile, place almonds in a dry skillet over medium heat and toast until golden in color and fragrant, about 5 to 10 minutes. Transfer to a plate and let cool.

Combine oranges, celery, yogurt, and lemon juice, stirring until well blended. Add chicken and refrigerate until ready to serve. Arrange salad greens in four individual salad bowls. Spoon ¼ of mixture over each, garnish with mandarin oranges, and top with the toasted almonds.

Serves 4.

MINI MEATBALLS with ANGEL HAIR PASTA

These small ground chicken meatballs demand a more delicate pasta, such as Angel Hair. Traditional tomato sauce would overpower this dish, but the lighter semi-sweet combination of chili sauce and grape jelly works beautifully. A fine do-ahead recipe, this is perfect for a dinner party or ladies' luncheon. Present with warm finger rolls and a simple salad of mesculin greens.

Ingredients

1 ½ pounds lean ground chicken

2 egg whites

½ cup fine dry bread crumbs

½ cup water

1 (12 ounce) bottle chili sauce

6 ounces grape jelly

2 tablespoons lemon juice

16 ounce package Angel Hair Pasta

1 tablespoon chopped flat leaf parsley

Procedure

In large bowl, combine ground chicken, egg whites, bread crumbs, and water. Mix until thoroughly blended. In a deep 3-quart casserole dish, combine chili sauce, grape jelly, lemon juice. Shape mixture into balls the size of a walnut; place in chili sauce mixture. Heat, covered, in microwave oven for 12 minutes. Stir. Heat, covered, in microwave oven an additional 8 minutes or until sauce bubbles and meatballs are cooked. Allow to cool and refrigerate overnight or at least 2 or 3 hours. Any fat will congeal on top, skim off.

cont...

When ready to serve, cook pasta according to package directions. While the pasta is cooking, reheat the sauce and meatballs. Drain pasta, transfer to a warm platter, and pour on sauce and meatballs. Scatter parsley over all.

Serves 4 to 6.

"And men sit down to that nourishment which is called supper."

—William Shakespeare

OVEN FRIED CHICKEN with RASPBERRY SAUCE

Lean chicken breasts, trimmed of any visible fat, contain barely a trace of saturated fat. Prepared in the following manner, this dish becomes cholesterol friendly and is the closest you can come to deep fried chicken that is safe and healthy. The sauce has a delightful whisper of raspberry flavor that marries well with the chicken.

Preheat oven to 350°

Ingredients

¾ cup Cheerios, crushed

¼ cup almonds, crushed

½ teaspoon sea salt

¼ teaspoon coarse ground black pepper

½ teaspoon dried tarragon

½ teaspoon sweet paprika

4 teaspoons olive oil

2 chicken breast halves, boneless, skinless, trimmed of any visible fat

Procedure

Mix together Cheerios, almonds, salt, pepper, tarragon, paprika, and 2 teaspoons of the olive oil. Place the chicken breasts in small baking pan. Spoon 1 teaspoon of the olive oil evenly over each breast. Completely cover tops of the breasts with the Cheerios mixture. Bake for 15 minutes or until juice runs clear when chicken is pierced with a fork. If juice is still pink, return to oven and bake an additional minute or so. Retest. Remove from pan and place on a warm platter. Set aside.

cont...

RASPBERRY SAUCE

Ingredients

1 cup store bought organic or homemade chicken broth, reserving ¼ cup

1 teaspoon raspberry jam

1 teaspoon cornstarch

1 teaspoon chopped flat parsley

Procedure

Place the baking pan on stovetop over medium heat. Use a spoon to scrape and brown crumbs and juice in the bottom of the pan. Pour in ¾ cup of the chicken broth and add the raspberry jam. In a small bowl, stir together briskly the remaining ¼ cup broth and the cornstarch to form a thick paste. Add the paste to the broth in the pan while stirring. As soon as the sauce starts to thicken, remove from heat and pour over the chicken. Scatter parsley over the top.

Serves 2.

"Why, sometimes I've believed as many as six impossible things before breakfast."

—Lewis Carroll

Jeannie Serpa

RACKLESS ROASTED CHICKEN

This is by far a superior method for roasting chicken. It is about as safe as one can get for cholesterol watchers who must monitor their intake of dangerous saturated fat, trans fat, and cholesterol. Baking over a layer of vegetables, rather than on a conventional wire rack, allows the chicken's juices to seep down over the vegetables, adding flavor and moisture. Roasting the chicken with vegetables in the same pan makes this an easy-to-prepare meal with only one pan to clean!

Preheat the oven to 350°

Ingredients

3 to 4 pound roasting chicken
Sea salt
2 peeled and halved sweet onions
3 large carrots, peeled and cut in large chunks
3 large red potatoes, unpeeled and quartered
2 tablespoons extra virgin olive oil
Freshly ground black pepper
2 whole lemons, washed in cold water
1 head garlic, unpeeled, cut in half
Paprika
Finely chopped flat leaf parsley

Preparation

As soon as you bring home the chicken, remove the giblets from inside the cavity and discard. Wash under cold running water inside and out. Pat dry with paper towels, including the cavity. Immediately discard those paper towels. Liberally salt the bird inside and out. Place in the refrigerator uncovered until ready to cook.

cont...

Procedure

Distribute the prepared vegetables closely in the bottom of a medium size roasting pan. Drizzle the olive oil over the vegetables and sprinkle with salt and pepper. Cut the lemons in half and place with garlic inside the cavity. Position the chicken with breast side up on top of your vegetable "rack." Tie the legs together with twine and tuck the wings under the bird. Rub the skin with a little olive oil.

Roast 1 to 1 ½ hours or until juices run clear when area between breast and thigh is pierced with a fork. If juices are still pink, return to oven for 10 minutes or until juices are clear. Remove from oven and allow the chicken to "rest" for 10 to 15 minutes.

Now comes the hard part. That golden brown crispy skin is loaded with saturated fat. Take a deep breath and skin that bird! Place on a large platter. Your roast won't look nearly as naked if you sprinkle it with paprika and chopped parsley. Surround with the roasted vegetables.

4 to 6 servings

SKILLET CHICKEN BREASTS
WITH APRICOT GRAVY

How often we think of coated skillet chicken as being cooked with breadcrumbs or cracker crumbs. Here's a cholesterol friendly alternative, one that adds a bit of soluble fiber from the Cheerios. Soluble fiber, remember, is what helps to clean out the built up layer of plaque that is lining our arteries and slowing down blood flow. Using olive oil helps too, since studies show that this "good" oil also helps in our battle against high cholesterol. Accompanying the chicken breasts is a quick and easy-to-fix flavored gravy that is poured as a sauce over the chicken.

Ingredients

¾ cup Cheerios, crushed

¼ cup walnuts, crushed

½ teaspoon sea salt

¼ teaspoon freshly ground black pepper

½ teaspoon dried thyme

½ teaspoon sweet paprika

1 cup skim milk

2 chicken breast halves, skinless and boneless

2 tablespoons extra virgin olive oil

Procedure

In a small bowl, combine the crushed Cheerios, walnuts, salt, pepper, thyme, and paprika.

Into a flat bottomed bowl or deep dish, pour the skim milk. Dip the breasts in the skim milk, being sure to moisten both sides, then dredge in the Cheerios mixture. Coat the breasts well on both sides and set aside.

Meanwhile, warm the oil in a heavy skillet over medium heat

cont...

and add the chicken. Cook until brown (about 3 minutes), turn and brown the other side for another 2 minutes or so. Reduce heat to low, cover, and continue cooking until chicken is cooked through and juice runs clear when the breasts are pierced with a fork. This could take as little as 5 minutes. If juice looks pink, cover and continue cooking for another minute or two. Remove to a warm plate.

APRICOT GRAVY

Ingredients

1 cup homemade or organic store bought chicken broth
1 heaping teaspoon apricot jam
1 teaspoon cornstarch

Procedure

Turn the heat under the skillet up to medium high. Scrape and brown any crumbs and juice in the bottom of the pan. Add ¾ of a cup of the broth, heat, and then stir in the jam.Combine thoroughly the reserved ¼ cup broth and cornstarch. Add this mixture to the broth and stir briskly for a minute until the broth thickens. Remove from heat immediately and pour over the chicken.

Serves 2.

Jeannie Serpa

TURKEY MEAT LOAF

At first glance, this recipe may appear long and complicated, but it comes together quickly. Be sure to ask your meat person for lean fresh-ly ground turkey. Unfortunately, fat is sometimes added to ground turkey to make it extra moist. Using the olive oil adds any needed mois-ture safely and effectively.

Preheat oven to 375°

Ingredients

4 fresh mushrooms, chopped

1 ½ tablespoons extra virgin olive oil

1 Vidalia or other sweet onion, chopped

1 large carrot, chopped

1 large celery stalk, chopped

2 garlic cloves, chopped

1 teaspoon fresh thyme leaves or ¼ teaspoon dried, crushed

2 tablespoons chopped fresh parsley or 2 teaspoons dried

Sea salt

Freshly ground black pepper

⅔ cup canned tomatoes, drain and reserve 2 tablespoons juice

1 tablespoon balsamic vinegar or red wine vinegar

1 tablespoon brown sugar

Dash or two of hot pepper sauce

1 ½ pounds lean ground turkey

½ cups breadcrumbs

1 egg

Canola cooking spray

cont...

Procedure

Clean mushrooms by rubbing gently with a damp dish towel. Do not clean in water as this will toughen them. Remove stems, chop and set aside.

Warm 1 tablespoon of the olive oil in a large heavy skillet over medium high heat. Add onion, carrot, celery, garlic, mushrooms, parsley, and thyme. Season to taste with salt and pepper. Sauté vegetables until tender crisp, about 6 minutes. Transfer to a medium size bowl and allow to cool slightly. Crush tomatoes slightly and combine with reserved juice, vinegar, brown sugar, and pepper sauce. Crumble the turkey with a fork and add to the tomato mixture along with the breadcrumbs and egg, combining well. Generously coat a loaf pan (approximately 8 ½ x 4 ½ inches) with the canola spray, add mixture, and brush the surface with remaining olive oil.

Bake on middle oven rack for about 1 hour or until loaf shrinks from sides of pan and top is golden brown. Let loaf stand for 10 minutes. Transfer to a warm platter. Cut into thick slices, spoon juices over the slices.

Serves 6.

"Strange to see how a good dinner and feasting reconciles everybody."

—Samuel Pepys

SEAFOOD

CAJUN SHRIMP over JASMINE RICE

Here is a Cajun dish with no saturated fat, yet it is high in flavor with a bit of fire. The shrimp provides omega-3 and the vegetables, of course, all help to control cholesterol.

Ingredients

2 cups jasmine rice
3 ½ cups cold water
2 teaspoons canola oil
1 teaspoon sea salt
3 tablespoons canola oil
¼ cup flour
1 cup chopped red bell pepper
1 cup chopped Vidalia or other sweet onion
½ cup peeled and chopped carrots
4 cloves garlic, minced
14 ounces vegetable broth, homemade or fat free store bought
1 (8 ounce) bottle clam juice
2 ½ pounds large size shrimp, peeled and deveined
1 teaspoon crushed red pepper flakes
1 teaspoon hot pepper sauce
½ cup chopped flat leaved Italian parsley

cont...

Procedure

Combine rice, water, canola oil, and salt in a saucepan. Bring to a boil, reduce heat, cover, and simmer for 15 minutes. Fluff with a fork and set aside.

Heat 3 tablespoons of canola oil in a heavy deep pot over medium heat. Add flour and cook, stirring over medium heat for 10 minutes or until the flour mixture is a deep golden brown. Add bell pepper, onion, carrots, and garlic. Cook, stirring, for about 5 minutes. Pour in the broth and clam juice, bring to a boil, reduce heat, and simmer for 10 minutes or until the vegetables are tender. Add shrimp, pepper flakes, and pepper sauce. Simmer all for 5-6 minutes or just until the shrimp are opaque. Ladle into bowls and top with rice. Garnish with parsley.

Serves 8.

CALAMARI SALAD with MUSHROOMS and AVOCADOS

Ingredients

2 slices fresh lemon

3 peppercorns or 1 teaspoon fresh ground black pepper

2 cloves garlic, unpeeled, but slightly crushed

¼ teaspoon sea salt

1 quart cold water

3 medium squid (calamari), cleaned and cut into rings

6-8 sprigs of parsley, finely chopped

2 tablespoons fresh lemon juice

1 clove garlic, chopped

⅓ cup extra virgin olive oil

2 tablespoons white wine vinegar

cont...

Sea salt to taste

Fresh ground black pepper to taste

2 ripe avocados

½ pound mushrooms

Curly green lettuce

Cherry tomatoes, halved

1 lemon, cut into wedges

Procedure

In a saucepan, combine lemon, peppercorns, garlic, salt, and water. Bring to a boil, reduce heat, and simmer 10 minutes, covered. Add squid rings and cook from 1-2 minutes or until tender. *Do not overcook, as they will turn tough and rubbery.* They will appear white when done. Remove squid, drain, and let cool. In a jar with a tight fitting lid place parsley, lemon juice, garlic, olive oil, vinegar, salt, and pepper. Shake vigorously.

Peel and cube the avocados. Cut off stems and slice the mushrooms. Add both, along with the squid, to a *glass* or *ceramic* bowl. Pour the dressing over all, toss gently, and allow to marinate at least one hour. Distribute the marinated mixture evenly on a platter over a bed of lettuce. Garnish with cherry tomato halves for added color and additional taste. Present with lemon wedges for squeezing over the salad at table.

Serves 4.

CRAB SALAD FINGER ROLLS

Crabmeat is rich in omega-3 fatty acids, which we know are cholesterol lowering. It is also free of saturated (bad) fat and trans fat. Reduced ("lite") mayonnaise is delicious and contains no saturated fat, no cholesterol, and no trans fat, whereas regular mayonnaise has 1.5 mg. of saturated fat in just one tablespoon.

Ingredients

14 ounces cooked crabmeat or imitation crab, chopped

¼ cup fat free or reduced fat mayonnaise

1 large stalk celery, chopped

1 tablespoon fresh lemon juice

1 teaspoon dried minced onion or fresh sweet

½ teaspoon dried dill weed or 1 ½ teaspoons fresh chopped

½ teaspoon dried parsley or 1 ½ teaspoons fresh chopped

Coarse ground black pepper

Sea salt to taste

6-8 finger rolls

Curly green lettuce

Procedure

Combine all ingredients and refrigerate to chill and allow the flavors to meld. When ready to serve, slit the rolls with a serrated knife, being careful not cut all the way through. Spread a thin coat of mayonnaise inside each roll, line with lettuce, and fill with crab salad.

CRABMEAT SALAD with LEMON CAPER DRESSING

Ingredients

15 ounces fresh cooked crabmeat or imitation crab

1 pound fresh asparagus

½ teaspoon sea salt

Iceberg lettuce

Lemon caper dressing

Paprika

Radishes

Procedure

If using fresh cooked crabmeat, drain and remove any cartilage or remaining shell. Flake the meat. If using imitation crab, simply remove from package and chop.

Wash asparagus and snap off tough ends, leaving tender spears only. Steam in a small amount of salted water on stovetop, covered, for 10 minutes or until tender crisp. You may cook in microwave oven, with 1 inch of salted water, covered, for 3 or 4 minutes.

Wash the lettuce and carefully pull off 6 "cups" of leaves. Place 3 or 4 asparagus spears in each cup, followed by ⅓ cup crabmeat. Cover with Lemon Caper Dressing and sprinkle liberally with paprika. Garnish with sliced radishes.

Serves 6.

LEMON CAPER DRESSING

Ingredients

½ cup fat free or reduced fat mayonnaise

1 tablespoon drained capers

1 tablespoon fresh lemon juice

½ teaspoon Dijon mustard

1 teaspoon Worcestershire sauce

Dash hot pepper sauce

Procedure

Combine all ingredients in a small bowl. Pour over crabmeat and asparagus just before serving.

DEEP FRIED CALAMARI in a BEER BATTER

You may have thought you could never again enjoy deep fried foods, but frying in canola oil provides a safe and excellent substitute for shortening or lard, which is nothing more than refined pig fat. Store bought or restaurant tartar sauce is usually made with mayonnaise that is high in saturated fat. Try this Mock Tartar. It is delicious!

Ingredients

1 can beer at room temperature

1 cup all purpose flour

1 teaspoon sea salt

1 teaspoon sweet paprika

cont...

½ teaspoon black pepper

3 pounds calamari (squid), cleaned and sliced into rings

Canola oil

Procedure

In a mixing bowl combine beer, flour, salt, paprika, and pepper. Pour oil into a deep pan or electric fryer and heat to 375°. Dip each squid ring into batter and let excess batter run off. Carefully ease each slice into the oil, being careful not to splatter and risk burning yourself. Remove as soon as brown (30 seconds to 1 minute). Fry the rings just a few at a time, allowing enough room. Calamari will toughen if overcooked. As you remove the squid, layer them on paper towels. They will remain crisp until all the rings are fried. Present with mock tartar sauce.

Serves four.

MOCK TARTAR SAUCE

Ingredients

½ cup reduced or fat free mayonnaise

½ cup fat free plain yogurt

3 tablespoons drained pickle relish

Procedure

In a small bowl combine mayonnaise, yogurt, and drained relish.

GOURMET TUNA ROLLS

No mayonnaise is needed in these tuna salad sandwiches. The hummus adds unbelievable flavor and moisture. The lemon and mint marry perfectly with the tuna, and garbanzo beans are high on the list of cholesterol fighters.

Ingredients

1 (6 ounce) can tuna fish packed in olive oil

1 tablespoon extra virgin olive oil

1 teaspoon red wine vinegar

1 tablespoon minced Vidalia or other sweet onion

2 tablespoons chopped black pitted olives

Fresh ground pepper to taste

1 ¾ cup garbanzo beans, drained and rinsed in cold water

2 cloves garlic, peeled

1 teaspoon lemon zest (grated lemon peel)

3 tablespoons fresh lemon juice

¼ cup mint leaves

4-6 good quality sandwich rolls

Procedure

Drain the tuna, flake finely with a fork, and place in a bowl. Add your own good olive oil. Mix in the vinegar, onion, and olives. Add pepper to taste and set aside. Make a hummus by placing garbanzos, garlic, lemon zest, lemon juice, and mint leaves in a food processor. Pulse a few times until the hummus is smooth. Split the rolls and spread each side with a generous coating of hummus. Add tuna salad and secure with toothpick. Serve these with Make Your Own Potato Chips and a few raw carrot sticks. Recipe for Make Your Own Potato Chips is in the APPETIZER section.

Makes 4-6 sandwiches.

Jeannie Serpa

LEMON PEPPER SWORDFISH,
BAKED or GRILLED

Whichever method you chose for preparing this succulent lemony swordfish, know that you are serving a high protein dish that's loaded with omega-3, a great cholesterol fighter. Handy tip: Roll lemon on your counter while pressing down hard. This releases the juice, resulting in twice the usual amount.

Ingredients

3 tablespoons store bought Lemon Hummus

1 teaspoon lemon zest (grated lemon peel)

1 teaspoon lemon juice

1 teaspoon minced sweet onion

1 teaspoon fresh ground black pepper

2 pounds swordfish

Sweet paprika

1 tablespoon olive oil

1 whole lemon

A few sprigs of flat leaf parsley

Grape or cherry tomatoes

Procedure

Combine hummus, zest, lemon juice, onion, and pepper.

TO BAKE: Preheat oven to 400°. Place swordfish in a baking dish and spread with the hummus mixture. Sprinkle with paprika. Bake 15-20 minutes or until cooked to your liking. Do not overcook or fish will be dry!

TO GRILL: Coat one side of fish with olive oil and place on grill

cont...

with oil side down. Spread the hummus mixture on the top side, sprinkle with paprika, and grill over medium heat 10-15 minutes or until cooked to your liking. Careful not to overcook or the swordfish will be dry!

Place fish on a platter and serve with lemon cut into wedges to be squeezed over the fish at the table. Garnish with plenty of parsley and tomatoes for color.

LOBSTER LINGUINE

A truly elegant way to serve pasta. All ingredients here are cholesterol friendly. This is a quick and easy special occasion or company dish and all that is needed to round it out is a simple green salad and warm dinner rolls.

Ingredients

3 tablespoons olive oil

1 clove garlic, minced

1 teaspoon nutmeg

1 teaspoon freshly ground black pepper

3 tablespoons prepared honey mustard

½ cup clam juice

⅔ cup cognac

2 cups cooked lobster meat, cut in bite size pieces

2 (16 ounce) packages linguine

Fresh lemon juice

Lemon wedges

cont...

Procedure

In a large skillet, warm oil over medium low heat and cook garlic until soft. Add nutmeg, pepper, mustard, clam juice, and cognac. Simmer for 1 or 2 minutes. (Most of the alcohol in the cognac will evaporate with cooking.) Gently fold in the lobster and continue to simmer over low heat until just heated through, about 5-10 minutes. Meanwhile, cook the linguine according to package directions.

Drain pasta and divide onto warm dinner plates. Remove lobster from the sauce with a slotted spoon and set aside on a warm plate. Pour sauce over pasta, toss slightly, and top with lobster. Drizzle with lemon juice and serve with extra lemon wedges on the side.

Yield: 8 servings

"Eat to live, don't live to eat."

—Jeannie Serpa

LOBSTERMAN'S PIE

Here is my elegant, sumptuous seafood version of Shepherd's Pie. I love, love, love this! It's an easy-to-prepare, do ahead, impress your guests, can't beat it presentation. It is hard to believe that anything that tastes this good could be cholesterol safe, yet it is.

Preheat oven to 350°

Ingredients

3 stalks celery, chopped

½ sweet onion, diced

1 tablespoon canola oil

1 pound cooked lobster meat, cut into large chunks

½ cup white wine (not cooking wine, use the good stuff)

1 teaspoon dried dill

1 pound package frozen baby sweet peas

1 teaspoon canola oil

Sea salt

Coarse ground black pepper

4-6 cups mashed potatoes (See recipe for Creamy Mashed Potatoes)*

Canola cooking spray or 2 tablespoons soft tub margarine, melted

Paprika

Procedure

In a large skillet, sauté celery and onion in the canola oil until tender crisp. Stir in lobster, wine, and dill. Remove from heat immediately.

cont...

Spread lobster mixture into a 9"x13" baking dish. Toss frozen peas with canola oil, salt, and pepper to taste. Layer over the lobster mixture.

Spread creamy mashed potatoes over all. Spray top of potatoes with canola cooking oil or pour over the melted margarine. Sprinkle evenly with paprika and bake for about 20 minutes or until heated through and golden brown. (Paprika acts as a browning agent and adds extra flavor).

Yield: 4-6 servings.

* See Vegetable section of cook book

MONKFISH with BASIL MAYONNAISE

Years ago monkfish was called Poor Man's Lobster because of its resemblance in texture to real lobster. It is a firm white fish and perfect for skewering. High in omega-3 and low in cholesterol, it is a good friend to those of us seeking to lower our cholesterol levels.

Ingredients

½ cup reduced fat mayonnaise

½ cup fat free plain yogurt

1 teaspoon dried or 1 tablespoon chopped fresh basil

¼ cup olive oil

1 clove garlic, minced

Sea salt to taste

Fresh ground black pepper

2 pounds monkfish

¾ cup olive oil

2 tablespoon fresh lemon juice

cont...

1 teaspoon minced fresh parsley

2 cloves garlic, minced

1 teaspoon sea salt

⅛ teaspoon fresh ground black pepper

½ teaspoon dried oregano

1 basket cherry tomatoes

Procedure

To make the Basil Mayonnaise, first combine the mayonnaise and yogurt. Add basil, olive oil, garlic, salt, and pepper. Refrigerate overnight or at least for an hour, allowing flavors to meld.

Cut monkfish into 1 ½ inch cubes. Whisk together the olive oil, lemon juice, parsley, garlic, salt, pepper, and oregano. Place monkfish in a shallow dish, pour over the olive oil mixture and toss to coat. Cover with plastic wrap and allow to marinate for 5-6 hours or overnight in the refrigerator.

Thread the fish alternated with tomatoes on skewers and grill or broil for about 3 minutes on each side. Spread with the basil mayonnaise.

Easily serves 4-6.

"He who loves his family, watches his cholesterol."

—Jeannie Serpa

MUSSELS STEAMED in WINE

Years ago mussels and other shellfish were thought to be too high in cholesterol for anyone with an elevated level. Today we know that shellfish, lobster, crabs, and other crustaceans actually help to lower cholesterol. Blue mussels, whose shells are dark blue or blackish in color, are sweeter than most other bivalves and considered a delicacy.

Ingredients

2 quarts mussels

3 tablespoons olive oil

1 medium Vidalia or other sweet onion, sliced thin

4 cloves garlic, peeled and crushed

4 celery stalks, peeled and chopped

8 ounces dry white wine

1 ¼ teaspoons dried thyme or 1 tablespoon chopped fresh

½ teaspoon dried parsley or 1 ½ teaspoons chopped fresh

Sourdough bread

Procedure

Purchase mussels whose shells are tightly closed. Discard any with open or "gaped" shells. Scrub with a stiff brush and remove threads. Heat olive oil in a large heavy pan with a cover. Add onion, garlic, celery and sauté until the onion is transparent. Add the mussels, pour wine over all, and cover. Cook over medium high heat 3-4 minutes, shaking the covered pan vigorously to combine ingredients. Remove from heat and let stand for 2 minutes. Remove cover and sprinkle with thyme and parsley. By now the mussels will have opened. Use a large slotted spoon to remove mussels and place them on a platter. Drain off the broth and pour over all. Serve with thick slices of bread for dipping.

Serves 4.

OPEN SALMON SALAD "SANDWICHES"

Salmon is high in omega-3 fatty acids, which are known to lower cholesterol. No need for salt here, since there is plenty in the mayonnaise. The lemon juice adds a bit of piquancy.

Ingredients

1 ½ cups leftover cooked salmon

1 teaspoon finely chopped sweet onion

1 tablespoon finely chopped celery

2 tablespoon reduced fat mayonnaise

½ teaspoon dried dill or 1 ½ tablespoons fresh chopped

2 teaspoons fresh lemon juice

Fresh ground pepper to taste

Rice cakes, lightly salted

Procedure

Flake salmon with a fork. Stir in onion, celery, mayonnaise, dill, lemon juice, and pepper. Add more mayonnaise, if needed. Spread the mixture on rice cakes and enjoy.

Makes 1 ¾ cups.

ROASTED CITRUS SALMON

Lemon, lime, and salmon combine well and bring a slight tartness to this easy-to-cook entrée. Whether for family or company, anyone who likes salmon will love this version. Even my daughter Mary Jane, who is not especially fond of fish, goes for a second helping. Serve with Almond Rice (this recipe can be found in the Vegetable and Side Dishes

cont...

Section of this book). Simply elegant! Ingredients known to lower cholesterol.

Preheat oven to 400°

Ingredients

- 1 tablespoon chopped fresh Italian parsley (substitute 1 teaspoon dried)
- 1 tablespoon chopped fresh dill (substitute 1 teaspoon dried)
- 2 teaspoons lemon zest
- 2 teaspoons lime zest
- 1 teaspoon sea salt (optional)
- ½ teaspoon coarse ground black pepper
- 1 salmon filet (about 2 ½ pounds, boneless with skin on)
- Paprika
- Lemon wedges
- Parsley

Procedure

Combine herbs, zests, salt, and pepper. Place salmon in pan, skin side down. Rub herb and zest mixture over salmon and coat liberally with paprika. Bake for 20 minutes or until fish flakes easily with a fork, yet is still moist.

Serve on a platter with lemon wedges. Garnish with parsley.

Yield: 4-6 servings.

SALMON CAKES

These time saving, savory salmon cakes are a perfect way to use left-overs. I deliberately cook extra salmon and mashed potatoes just so I can make them. Here's a quick and easy method to provide a cholesterol lowering meal for you and your family or guests. No need for salt in this recipe since the potatoes and salmon are already seasoned.

Ingredients

1 cup flaked cooked fresh salmon (leftovers are fine)

1 cup creamy mashed potatoes (leftovers or see recipe in Vegetable and Side Dishes section)

2 teaspoons fresh lemon juice

½ teaspoon dried dill weed or 1 ½ teaspoon fresh dill

1 teaspoon dried minced onion or 1 tablespoon fresh, finely chopped onion

Coarsely ground black pepper to taste

2 tablespoons extra virgin olive oil

Paprika

Procedure

Combine the first six ingredients in a bowl. Be sure your creamy mashed potatoes have been prepared using my low cholesterol method found in the Vegetable and Side Dishes section of this book. Form 2 large patties (cakes). Heat 2 tablespoons oil in a frying pan, add the cakes, and sprinkle liberally with paprika. Sauté over medium/low heat until golden brown on the underside. Turn and cook until golden brown and heated through.

Serves 2.

SCROD with WINE ROSEMARY DEMI GLAZE

This recipe will transform everyday white fish into an elegantly scrumptious company entrée. Who will guess that your intent is to serve a low cholesterol dish high in omega-3? Accompany this with fresh asparagus, sliced vine ripened tomatoes, and a nutty rice pilaf. Complement with chilled white wine and bow graciously to the applause!

Preheat oven to 400°

Ingredients

2 pounds scrod, cod, or haddock, skinless and boneless

Dijon mustard

Seasoned bread crumbs

2 cups white wine (not cooking wine, use the good stuff!)

¼ cup soft tub margarine, low in saturated fat

Sea salt

Freshly ground black pepper

2 cloves fresh garlic

2 sprigs fresh rosemary

Additional rosemary for garnish

Procedure

Lightly coat both sides of the fish with Dijon mustard and sprinkle with bread crumbs. Place on a baking sheet and bake for 15-20 minutes or until the fish flakes easily with a fork yet is still moist and succulent in the center.

While the fish is cooking, make the sauce. Pour the wine into a saucepan and bring to a boil over medium high heat. Lower heat and simmer until wine is reduced by one half its volume. Add

cont...

margarine and season with salt and pepper. Now add the garlic and rosemary to the pan and simmer for 5-7 minutes. Strain this sauce into another pan and keep warm. When ready to serve, drizzle over the fish. Garnish with rosemary.

Serves 4-6.

Food Fact: *The banana, together with its relative the plantain, is the most consumed fruit in the world.*

SPEEDY MICROWAVE SALMON, #1

Who says you can't microwave fish? This recipe is both fast and delicious. The salmon stays moist, your kitchen will not end up smelling "fishy," and you will save precious time! Ingredients known to lower cholesterol? Salmon with its high omega-3 content, olive oil, and garbanzo beans (the main ingredient in hummus).

Ingredients

Four 6 ounce salmon filets, boneless with skin on

4 teaspoons extra virgin olive oil

4 teaspoons fresh lemon juice

1 (7 ounce) container store bought lemon hummus

Coarse ground black pepper

Paprika

Procedure

Arrange salmon skin side down in a microwavable casserole dish with cover. Spread 1 teaspoon olive oil and 1 teaspoon lemon juice over each filet. Spread hummus on top (about ¼ inch thick). Sprinkle *generously* with pepper and paprika. Cover, tipping the lid slightly to allow venting.

Microwave ovens vary, so start with cooking 5 minutes on high. It is important not to overcook. The fish should flake easily with a fork, yet still be succulently moist inside. Serve this with Creamy Mashed Potatoes and Roasted Brussels Sprouts*.

Serves 4

* For recipes see Vegetable and Side Dishes Section in cookbook

SPEEDY MICROWAVE SALMON, #2

My daughter claimed she didn't like salmon until she tried this version. I strongly urge you to try both versions of the microwaved salmon.

Ingredients

2 (6 ounce) salmon filets, boneless with skin on

2 teaspoons extra virgin olive oil

2 teaspoons fresh lemon juice

Sea salt

Dill

Coarse ground black pepper

Paprika

Procedure

Place salmon with the skin side down in a small microwavable casserole dish with cover.

Spread each filet with 1 teaspoon of olive oil and lemon juice. Sprinkle lightly with salt and generously with pepper, dill, and lastly with paprika. Cover, tipping the lid slightly to allow for venting.

Microwave ovens vary, so start with cooking 4 minutes on high. It is important not to overcook. The fish should flake easily with a fork, yet still be succulently moist inside.

Serves 2.

SWORDFISH in SOUR CREAM MUSHROOM SAUCE

Here's a savory method for preparing swordfish that will delight family and guests. Because of its bland color, this dish deserves to be served with colorful vegetables such as carrots, beets, or red bell peppers. Helpful tip: Cook swordfish roughly ten minutes per inch of thickness.

Ingredients

½ pound fresh mushrooms

4 tablespoons canola oil

6 shallots, finely chopped

⅓ cup dry white wine

2 pounds swordfish, roughly 1 inch thick

Sea salt to taste

Freshly ground black pepper to taste

1 ½ cups fat free sour cream

Watercress

Procedure

Clean the mushrooms by wiping them with a damp cloth, then slice. (Cleaning them in water will toughen them.) Add canola oil to a large heavy skillet and sauté mushrooms and shallots until soft. Remove them with a slotted spoon and set aside.

Add wine to the mushroom liquid in the pan. Season the swordfish with salt and pepper then place in the pan. Cook approximately 4 minutes on each side. Spoon sour cream over the steaks. Surround the steaks with mushrooms and shallots and continue cooking for 2 more minutes or until done to your liking. *Do not overcook or the fish will be dry.* Move the swordfish to a warm platter and pour the sauce over all. Garnish with watercress.

Serves 4-6.

TOMATO DRESSED COD over PASTA

Here is a tasty marriage of wholesome flavor and cholesterol lowering ingredients. By repeating the cod's seasoning in the pasta, the flavors come together in perfect harmony. Serve this with a green salad and thick slices of Italian bread.

Preheat oven to 400°

Ingredients

1 pound cod (boneless and skinless)

2 teaspoons extra virgin olive oil

2 teaspoons fresh lemon juice

Sea salt

Fresh ground black pepper

2 medium red ripe tomatoes

2 teaspoons minced sweet onion or ½ teaspoon dried onion flakes

½ teaspoon dried basil or 1½ teaspoons chopped fresh

¼ teaspoon dried oregano or ¾ teaspoon chopped fresh

PASTA

10 ounces spaghetti or linguine

1 tablespoon extra virgin olive oil

1 teaspoon dried basil or 1 tablespoon chopped fresh

½ teaspoon dried oregano or 1½ teaspoons chopped fresh

Garlic salt to taste

Fresh ground pepper to taste

cont...

Procedure

Place cod in a baking dish (about 2 inches deep). Distribute olive oil and lemon juice over the fish and sprinkle with salt and pepper. Slice tomatoes and arrange over the fish, overlapping slightly. Sprinkle with onion, basil, and oregano. Bake about 15-20 minutes. Halfway through cooking, spoon juices over all. Fish is cooked when it flakes easily with a fork, yet is still moist and succulent in the center.

While cod is baking, cook pasta according to package directions. Drain pasta, toss with 1 tablespoon of olive oil, basil, oregano, garlic salt, and pepper. Plate the pasta and arrange the cod with tomato topping on top. Spoon pan juices over all.

Serves 4.

TROPICAL LOBSTER SALAD

The old idea that lobster, shrimp, scallops, oysters, and other shellfish were bad for our cholesterol has been dispelled. Those early measurements were inaccurate and today we know that many shellfish actually have a very low cholesterol content. Be wary, however, of the butter, sour cream, and other fat laden accompaniments that are traditionally served with shellfish. This recipe is a fine example of a savory dish that is refreshing and free of harmful ingredients.

Ingredients

2 lobsters, about 2 pounds each

2 teaspoons white wine vinegar

1 tablespoon fat free sour cream

½ cup olive oil

1 teaspoon Dijon mustard

cont...

½ teaspoon dried tarragon or 1 ½ teaspoons chopped fresh

Sea salt to taste

Freshly ground black pepper to taste

1 ripe papaya, peeled, seeded, and cubed

2 kiwi, peeled and cubed

1 bunch watercress, stemmed and chopped

Procedure

To cook the lobsters:

Plunge the lobsters into a huge pot of boiling water, headfirst. Cover, boil for about 10-12 minutes or until the shells turn bright red. Remove from pot and allow to cool slightly.

To remove meat from shell, first twist off the claws. Crack each claw with a nutcracker, hammer, or what have you. Remove meat and set aside. Separate the tail-piece from the body by arching the back until it cracks. Bend the tail back and break the flippers off the tail-piece. Insert a fork where the flippers broke off and push the meat through. Set aside to cool.

Dressing

Combine vinegar, sour cream, olive oil, mustard, tarragon, salt, and pepper. Chop the lobster into bite size chunks and marinate in the dressing overnight. Just before serving, gently fold in the papaya, kiwi, and watercress.

Serves 6-8.

ZESTY BAKED FLOUNDER

We all know people who douse their fish with ketchup to give it flavor and color. This savory entrée is bursting with flavor and its color is enhanced by the garnish. A great tasting "company" dish to serve with pride. Substitute sole, cod, or any mild white fish for the flounder. Thicker fillets require increased baking time (15-20 minutes).

Preheat oven to 450°

Ingredients

3 tablespoons fat free plain yogurt

½ teaspoon Dijon mustard

1 tablespoon fresh grated ginger or ¼ teaspoon powdered

2 teaspoons prepared horseradish

2 teaspoons brown sugar

4 teaspoons low sodium soy sauce

1 clove garlic, minced

2 six ounce flounder filets

Canola cooking spray

¼ cup bread crumbs

3 cherry tomatoes, halved (optional)

1 tablespoon chopped flat leaf parsley

Procedure

Combine yogurt and mustard in a small bowl. Stir in ginger, horseradish, sugar, soy sauce, and garlic. Brush this mixture on both sides of the filets. Place the fish in a shallow baking pan which has been coated with cooking spray. Sprinkle with breadcrumbs. Then spray the bread crumbs with canola. Bake

cont...

10-15 minutes or until fish flakes easily with a fork. Do not over-bake.

Plate the fish and surround with the halved tomatoes, cut side down. Sprinkle over all with parsley.

Serves 2. You may double or triple the recipe and bake the prepared flounder on a sprayed cookie sheet. Baking time will be about the same.

"I shall content myself with merely declaring my conviction that, for the seeker who would live in the fear of God and would see him face to face, restraint in diet both as to quantity and quality is as essential as restraint in thought and speech."

—Mahatma Gandhi

Vegetables

&

Side Dishes

ALMOND RICE

Almonds are an excellent source of vitamin E and are rich in monoun-saturated fat (good fat). Monounsaturated fat helps to lower LDL and raise HDL. 80% of the world's almonds are grown in California.

Preheat oven to 350°

Ingredients

1 ½ cups of long grain rice

3 ⅓ cups water

1 teaspoon canola oil

½ teaspoon salt

Coarse ground pepper to taste

½ cup slivered almonds

Procedure

Prepare rice according to package directions, using canola oil in place of butter. While rice is cooking, place almonds on an ungreased cookie sheet and toast in the oven for about ten minutes or until golden brown and fragrant. As an alternative you may wish to toast the almonds in a dry skillet on your stove top. Toss almonds and pepper with the rice.

Serves 6.

BAKED POTATOES with AVOCADO TOPPING

Baked potatoes are not fattening, nor do they contain cholesterol or dangerous fats. It's the butter and sour cream that make them dangerous for the high cholesterol patient. Avocados help reduce cholesterol. Canadian bacon has one quarter of the fat of regular bacon. Cooking it until crisp and blotting it removes virtually all saturated (bad) fat.

Preheat oven to 425°

Ingredients

4 large Idaho or Russet potatoes

4 slices Canadian bacon, cut in ½ inch pieces

1 ripe Haas avocado

Juice of 1 lime

2 tablespoons fat free sour cream

1 teaspoon chopped fresh cilantro

1 or 2 green scallions, finely chopped

Procedure

Scrub potatoes, prick skin a few times with a fork. Place in oven and set timer for one hour.

In a dry skillet, fry the bacon over medium heat until crisp. Transfer to a plate and blot any excess fat with a paper towel. Set aside.

Remove potatoes from oven. Cut a cross on the top of each potato and press down to open up. Just before serving, spoon a dollop of Avocado Topping on each and sprinkle with bacon and onions.

Serves 4.

cont...

AVOCADO TOPPING

Procedure

Halve the avocado, leave skin intact, and remove pit. With a teaspoon, scoop out the flesh and place in a small bowl. Sprinkle each piece with lime juice. The lime juice adds piquancy and keeps the avocados from turning brown. Slice avocado into a food processor. Add cilantro and sour cream. Process until creamy and transfer to a small bowl.

BAKED POTATOES with PINK CHEESE SAUCE

Preheat oven to 425°

Ingredients

1 cup Yogurt Cheese
3 teaspoons ketchup
2 teaspoons chopped chives or ½ teaspoon dried onion flakes
4 medium baking potatoes

Preparation

Make the Yogurt Cheese (see recipe on page 50) the night before or at least an hour in advance. To make the Pink Cheese Topping, simply add ketchup and chives. Refrigerate until serving time.

cont...

Procedure

Scrub potatoes, wipe dry, and prick the skin a few times with a fork. Bake for one hour. Test by squeezing. They will feel soft when cooked. Remove from oven, cut open, and top with Pink Cheese Sauce. Serve extra sauce in a small bowl on the side.

Serves 4.

BAKED POTATOES with SASSY TOPPING

Here's a tasty alternative to those baked potatoes smothered in butter. A single tablespoon of butter contains 2 full grams of saturated fat, the "bad" fat that we're trying to avoid. The sassy sauce topping is an innocent looking coral pink in color, but don't be fooled. Depending on the amount of pepper sauce you use, it can pack quite a wallop. The amount used here produces a fairly mild topping.

Preheat oven to 425°

Ingredients

4 large Idaho, Russet, or other baking potatoes

½ cup fat free plain yogurt

½ cup fat free sour cream

4 teaspoons ketchup

2 or 3 dashes hot pepper sauce, according to taste

1 clove garlic, minced

1 teaspoon minced dried onion flakes or 1 tablespoon minced fresh onion

1 tablespoon grated parmesan cheese

4 teaspoons canola oil

4 teaspoons fresh lemon juice

cont...

Celery salt (optional)

Freshly coarse ground black pepper

Procedure

Scrub potatoes, wipe dry, and pierce a few times with a fork. Bake for 1 hour or until potato feels soft when squeezed.

Combine yogurt, sour cream, ketchup, pepper sauce, garlic, onion, and cheese. Refrigerate while potatoes are baking, allowing the flavors to blend. Cut a cross in the top of each potato and squeeze to open up. Add 1 teaspoon canola oil and 1 teaspoon lemon juice to each potato. Serve the sassy topping on the side, along with celery salt and extra pepper sauce.

"Tell me what you eat and I'll tell you what you are."

—Anthelme Brillat-Savarin

BAKED RICE

Quick and easy to assemble, this excellent side dish can be baking while you see to the rest of the meal. This is a savory accompaniment to seafood or poultry and makes a perfect presentation when served with colorful vegetables such as beets and peas. Make your meals eye appealing and don't forget the garnish!

Preheat oven to 350°

Ingredients

1 cup rice

1 (10.5 ounce) can fat free beef or chicken broth

½ cup water

1 tablespoon fresh lemon juice

1 tablespoon minced onion

½ teaspoon Fines Herbs

2 tablespoons soft tub margarine (never use stick margarine)

1 tablespoon chopped chives or parsley

Procedure

Combine rice, broth, water, lemon juice, onion, and Fines Herbs. There is no need for salt in this recipe since the broth will have plenty. Place in a casserole dish and dot with margarine. Bake for 1 hour, stirring halfway through. Garnish with chives or parsley.

Serves 4-6.

BAKED STUFFED POTATOES

Who says you must avoid stuffed potatoes when trying to control your blood cholesterol count? These contain a small amount of saturated (bad) fat from the margarine. Since they seem to taste just as good without margarine, skip it if you have concerns.

Preheat oven to 425°

Ingredients

2 large Idaho or Russet potatoes
Small (8 ounces) container fat free sour cream
Fat free half & half cream
Sea Salt
Coarse ground black pepper
2 teaspoons chopped chives
4 teaspoons soft tub margarine, divided
Paprika
1 tablespoon finely chopped fresh flat leaf parsley for garnish

Procedure

Scrub potatoes, wipe dry, and prick a few times with a fork. Bake for one hour. Remove from oven. Do not cool, cut in half lengthwise while still hot (this will release steam and keep the skins crisp and firm). Carefully scoop out inside of each potato, reserve skins, and set aside. Place potatoes in a bowl. Mash with a fork or potato masher. Since potatoes differ in moisture, the amounts of sour cream and half & half cream that you add will vary. Start adding a little of each, beating with an electric mixer until extra creamy and moist. Season to taste with salt and pepper. Stir in chives. Spoon the mixture into the skin halves, heaping up in the center. Dust liberally with paprika and top each with one teaspoon of margarine. Preheat broiler or toaster oven.

cont...

A few minutes before serving time, place under heat and toast until golden brown. If desired, an additional teaspoon of margarine may be added. Garnish with parsley.

Serves 4.

BROCCOLI FLORETS, ROASTED with PECANS

Soluble fiber, omega-3, vitamin C, plus monounsaturated oil. They're all here in this tasty, unique way to cook broccoli. The lemon here lends a little piquancy, the pepper flakes a little zing. Celery salt is an important finishing touch.

Preheat oven to 425°

Ingredients

1 (14 ounce) package frozen broccoli baby florets
2 tablespoons extra virgin olive oil
Juice of half a lemon*
Coarse sea salt (Kosher salt)
Coarse ground black pepper
Pinch crushed red pepper flakes
¼ cup pecan or walnut pieces
Celery salt

Remember to roll the lemon on the counter top with the palm of your hand. It will release twice as much juice.

cont...

232

Procedure

Spread florets out on a cookie sheet. Distribute olive oil and lemon juice over all and stir until well coated. Sprinkle lightly with salt and black pepper. Add red pepper flakes and pecans and stir again. Distribute evenly and roast for 10 minutes for tender broccoli, 15 minutes for slightly toasted. Remove from oven and immediately sprinkle lightly with celery salt.

BUTTERLESS BAKED POTATOES

For years I ate my baked potatoes smothered in butter and loaded with salt and pepper. When I was told my blood cholesterol was extremely high, I invented this alternative. I've prepared my baked potatoes this way for so long that I no longer miss the butter. (Well, almost never.)

Ingredients

4 large baking potatoes

Celery salt

Canola oil

Juice from 1 lemon, freshly squeezed

Coarse ground black pepper

Paprika (optional)

Chopped chives (optional)

Sea salt and coarse ground black pepper

cont...

Procedure

Preheat oven to 425°

Scrub potatoes and prick a few times with a fork. Bake for one hour or until potatoes feel soft when squeezed. Remove from oven and immediately cut open. (This will allow steam to escape and keep the skins crisp.) Use a fork to slightly break up the inside and sprinkle lightly with celery salt. Distribute one or two teaspoons canola oil over each potato. Potatoes vary in moisture so judge accordingly. Add about 1 teaspoon of lemon juice to each. Sprinkle with paprika and chives for additional flavor and color. Add salt and pepper to taste. Plan to eat the skins. They're delicious served this way and are an excellent source of potassium, vitamin C, and vitamin B-6.

Serves 4.

CHANTILLY POTATOES

Years ago, before I was aware of the dangers of high cholesterol, I made these potatoes with lots of butter, whole milk, and high fat sour cream. The topping, of course, was whipped heavy cream! Today, I serve this much safer but still delicious version. These are special fare, perfect for dinner parties and festive occasions.

Ingredients

2 pounds potatoes

½ teaspoon salt

⅓ cup skim milk or fat free half & half cream

2 tablespoons soft tub margarine

⅓ cup fat free sour cream

2 tablespoons finely chopped chives

cont...

⅛ teaspoon coarse ground black pepper

Additional salt, if needed

Canola cooking spray or soft tub margarine

8 ounce container fat free Cool Whip

Grated Parmesan cheese

Paprika

Procedure

Peel and cut potatoes into roughly one inch chunks. Place in pot and cover with cold water; add salt. Bring to a boil over high heat. Reduce heat, cover, and continue cooking for 15 minutes or until potatoes are soft. Drain.

Set oven to 350°.

Return potatoes to pot, add skim milk and margarine. Use an electric beater on lowest speed to "mash." Add sour cream, and whip with speed on low to medium until potatoes are light and fluffy. Add more milk if needed. (You may opt to mash with a potato masher and whip with a large whisk.) Fold in the chives and add black pepper. Taste test and adjust seasonings.

Coat an oven proof casserole dish with canola spray or margarine and add the potato mixture. Spread about ½ inch of Cool Whip over the top, sprinkle lightly with Parmesan, and generously with paprika. Bake for 15 to 20 minutes or until potatoes are heated through.

Serves 6-8.

CREAMY MASHED POTATOES

We all love mashed potatoes and we all know that potatoes are good for us. It's what we add to those potatoes that make them fattening and high in cholesterol. By using fat free milk and sour cream with soft tub margarine (which is low in saturated fat, trans fat and cholesterol), we can make these yummy potatoes delicious and cholesterol friendly.

Ingredients

2 pounds potatoes (about 3 large Russet or Idaho)

1 teaspoon salt

2 tablespoons soft tub margarine

⅛ teaspoon celery salt

⅓ cup fat free sour cream

⅓ cup skim milk

1 tablespoon minced green onion (optional)

¼ teaspoon coarse ground black pepper

Additional salt to taste

Procedure

Peel and cut up potatoes into roughly 1 inch cubes. Place in pan, cover with cold water.

Add salt and bring to a boil over high heat. Lower heat, cover, and continue cooking until the potatoes are fork tender (approximately 15-20 minutes). Drain and return potatoes to pan.

In the same pan, add margarine to the potatoes and mash with a potato masher. Mix in celery salt, sour cream, and milk, whipping with a fork or heavy whisk until creamy and fluffy. You may use an electric beater instead. Not quite creamy enough? Adjust with a small amount of sour cream and milk to desired consistency. Add salt and pepper, if needed. Fold in green onions, adjust seasonings and serve piping hot.

Yield: 6 servings.

CUCUMBER BOATS

These are perfect as a crunchy, healthful snack or to take on a picnic.

Ingredients

2 cucumbers
½ cup fat free cream cheese
¼ cup peanut butter
¼ cup chopped peanuts

Procedure

Peel the cucumbers and cut in half lengthwise. Scoop out the seeds and set aside. Do not discard. Combine cheese and peanut butter in a bowl. Add the cucumber seeds and peanuts. Fill the cucumber halves (boats) with this mixture. If not using immediately, wrap in plastic wrap and refrigerate.

Serves 4.

"I live on good soup and not fine words."

—Molière

GREEN BEANS with PINE NUTS

Though we usually think of almonds as the perfect accompaniment to green beans, my family prefers this welcome change. Antioxidants from the beans along with the cholesterol reducing properties of pine nuts and olive oil place this offering high on my list of recommendations. Pine nuts are actually the tasty seeds of certain pine trees.

Ingredients

1 pound fresh green beans
½ cup pine nuts
2 tablespoons olive oil
Coarse sea salt or Kosher salt
Coarse ground black pepper

Procedure

Trim the green beans and cut into one inch pieces. Cover with cold salted water and bring to a boil. Reduce heat and simmer for 15-20 minutes or until tender. Drain and set aside.

Meanwhile, toast the pine nuts in a dry skillet over medium heat until golden brown and fragrant (5-10 minutes). You may skip this step if you're short on time, but include it if possible. Toasting really enhances the flavor.

Heat olive oil in a separate skillet, and add the beans, pine nuts, salt, and pepper. Toss gently over medium heat until beans are hot and well coated with oil. Adjust seasonings.

Serves 4.

GRILLED RADICCHIO

These ruby red heads, sometimes called red chicory or Italian chicory, have a pleasant peppery taste. Uncooked and sliced, they add a bit of punch and color to coleslaw and salad. Their flavor is too powerful to use uncooked on their own. Full of antioxidants and high on my list of cholesterol lowering vegetables, these are winners.

Ingredients

2 heads radicchio (pronounced ra-DEE-kee-o)

Extra virgin olive oil

Sea salt

Procedure

Wash and remove any wilted outer leaves. Cut in half from top to bottom (not across).

Brush the cut side with olive oil and sprinkle with salt. No need to add pepper. Cooking mellows their flavor, so grill the oiled halves cut side down over medium heat with cover closed for about 15 minutes. If you prefer, roast them uncovered with cut side up in the oven at 400° for 20-25 minutes, depending on size. Check from time to time during cooking. These should be tender-crisp, not mushy.

Serves 4.

GRILLED SUMMER VEGETABLES
with BALSAMIC VINAIGRETTE

This side dish is easy to prepare, colorful, and so tasty! The vegetables provide soluble fiber, which helps clean out clogged arteries, as well as vitamin C, vitamin E, and beta carotene. Serve it hot or chill leftovers and use as a salad. Remember, if you must occasionally use cheese, a little grated parmesan is your best bet.

Ingredients

2 medium size yellow summer squash, unpeeled

2 medium size zucchini, unpeeled

1 Vidalia onion, peeled and sliced

1 red bell pepper, seeded and cut in large pieces

1 green bell pepper, seeded and cut in large pieces

2 tablespoons extra virgin olive oil

Sea salt

⅛ teaspoon coarse black pepper

1 tablespoon grated parmesan cheese (optional)

Procedure

Cut squashes in half crosswise, then lengthwise. Combine squashes, onion, and peppers in a large bowl. Toss with 2 tablespoons olive oil, salt, and pepper. Grill, uncovered, over medium high heat for 10-12 minutes or until tender, turning once. Place in a large deep serving dish, add the vinaigrette, and toss gently. Sprinkle lightly with cheese.

Serves 4-6.

BALSAMIC VINAIGRETTE

Ingredients

2 tablespoons extra virgin olive oil
1 tablespoon balsamic vinegar
¼ cup chopped fresh basil

Procedure

Whisk together oil, vinegar, and basil.

"You don't have to cook fancy or complicated masterpieces—just good food from fresh ingredients."

—Julia Child

Jeannie Serpa

HURRY UP BAKED BEANS

In the mood for baked beans but no time for all that soaking and slow baking? We know that beans are high on the list of cholesterol reducing foods but did you know that even some canned baked beans are free of saturated fat, free of trans fat, and low in cholesterol? Enjoy this quick version that starts with Campbell's baked beans.

Preheat oven to 350°

Ingredients

11 ounce can Campbell's Pork and Beans

3 tablespoons catsup

1 tablespoon brown sugar

1 medium size carrot, shredded

1 stalk celery, small diced

½ teaspoon dried minced onion

1 clove garlic, minced

½ teaspoon coarse ground black pepper

Procedure

Remove the tiny piece of pork that is sometimes found on top of canned beans. Mix together all ingredients, plop in a one quart baking dish and bake 30 minutes. That's it!

Yield: 3 servings.

Variation

Remove baked beans from oven and add one cup of hot cooked rice. This magic combination of beans and rice produces a complete protein. Use as a main dish. Delicious and fulfilling served with a green salad.

LEGAL HOME FRIES

Potatoes are a good source of vitamins C and B-6, as well as potassium and other minerals. Not only are they inexpensive, filling, and nutritious but their flavor complements most foods. They are also low in calories (90 calories in a medium size potato). Cooking home fries in shortening adds calories, saturated fat, and trans fat. This method uses olive oil (a safe oil).

Ingredients

2 tablespoons olive oil

2 tablespoons chopped onion

4 cups chopped cooked red bliss potatoes, unpeeled

1 tablespoon chopped fresh parsley

Coarse sea salt to taste

Coarsely ground black pepper to taste

Procedure

Heat olive oil in a skillet over medium heat and sauté onions until they are transparent.

Add potatoes and parsley. Cook until hot, stirring occasionally. If your potatoes were cooked in salted water, additional salt may not be needed.

Serves 4-6.

MASHED POTATOES
with CARAMELIZED ONION

Guests coming for dinner? Need a great tasting vegetable that's simple, but with a new twist? Preparation time for this is only ten minutes; cooking time barely thirty. Flavor is high. This sounds as though it should be on the dangerous food list, but the low fat margarine along with the fat free cream make this a safe and savory company dish.

Ingredients

1 ½ pounds small Red Bliss potatoes, unpeeled and quartered

1 teaspoon salt

1 tablespoon low fat soft tub margarine

1 cup Vidalia or any sweet onion, large chop

1 tablespoon sugar

⅔ cup fat free half & half cream (I like Land o'Lakes)

1 teaspoon salt

¼ teaspoon coarsely ground black pepper

Procedure

Place potatoes in a saucepan, cover with cold water, add salt, bring to a boil, and reduce heat. Simmer fourteen minutes or until tender. Drain.

While the potatoes are cooking, caramelize the onions. Melt margarine in a nonstick skillet over low heat. Add onions. Stir frequently and add the sugar to aid in the caramelizing process. Cook until golden. Set aside.

Add cream, salt, and pepper to potatoes. Mash with a potato masher and fluff with a fork, or beat briefly with an electric beater. Fold in the onions. Oh, so good!

Serves 6.

MICROWAVE SPROUTS

In a hurry? Try these. The seasoning here imparts a fresh new taste to Brussels sprouts. Use margarine in place of butter. Keep in mind the fact that soft tub margarine is much lower in saturated (bad) fat than stick margarine.

Ingredients

1 pound Brussels sprouts

1 tablespoon soft tub low fat margarine

2 teaspoons fresh lemon juice

½ teaspoon dried dill

A sprinkle of garlic powder, according to taste

Salt and pepper to taste

Procedure

Prepare the sprouts by washing in cold water. Drain and remove any tough outer leaves. Halve oversized sprouts. Place everything in a microwavable covered bowl with the lid slightly tilted. Microwave ovens vary so cook on high for two minutes, then check. Sprouts should be tender crisp. If necessary, return to oven and cook an additional thirty seconds. Stir to distribute the melted margarine and serve.

Serves 4.

MICROWAVE ORANGE CARROTS

A bright and cheery addition to any meal, these cholesterol friendly carrots have two fringe benefits: #1 they are packed with vitamin A and #2 they contain beta carotene. Raw carrots are good for us, but beta carotene develops with the cooking. Actually, there's a third fringe benefit. They are delicious!

Ingredients

1 pound carrots, peeled and sliced diagonally

1 clementine, sectioned or ½ cup mandarin oranges, drained

1 heaping tablespoon frozen orange juice concentrate

¼ cup cold water

Sea salt and coarse ground black pepper to taste

Procedure

Combine all ingredients in a covered microwavable casserole dish. Cook on high with lid slightly tilted for 5-8 minutes. Microwave ovens vary, so best to test with a fork at 5 minutes. The carrots should be tender but not mushy.

MINTED CHICKPEAS

The addition of mint gives this dish a decidedly Greek flair. I had been cooking this for years, always using basil as the herb. At the suggestion of my New Hampshire friend, Hope, I switched to mint and love the unique flavor.

Ingredients

- 1 tablespoon extra virgin olive oil
- 1 large sweet onion
- Sea salt and coarse black pepper
- 1 clove garlic, chopped
- 1 (15.5 ounce) can garbanzo beans (chickpeas), drained and rinsed in cold water
- 1 (14.5 ounce) can diced tomatoes with juice
- 1 tablespoon dried mint (or substitute ¼ cup fresh chopped)

Procedure

In a large skillet, heat oil over medium heat. Halve the onion, peel, and slice thin.

Add to skillet and cook until soft. Add salt and pepper to taste, then stir in the garlic, chickpeas, and tomatoes. Simmer all this for about 8 minutes, stirring occasionally.

Remove from heat and add mint.

Cover and allow to stand for 5 minutes so the flavors have a chance to marry. If you would like to try this with basil instead of mint, use 1 teaspoon dried basil and ½ teaspoon dried oregano.

ORANGE GLAZED BEETS

Most glazed beets call for butter. Here is a cholesterol safe way to achieve results without sacrificing flavor. Beets are a colorful addition to an otherwise bland looking dinner plate and are rich in antioxidants. These are a bit sweet, so taste test before adding the marmalade. You may wish to skip the marmalade.

Ingredients

1 tablespoon olive oil

3 cups sliced fresh cooked or jarred beets

¼ cup white wine vinegar

¼ cup orange juice

¼ cup sugar

1 tablespoon orange marmalade

Procedure

Warm olive oil in a large skillet, drain beets, and add to pan. Stir in vinegar and orange juice. Cook until heated through, then add the sugar, tossing gently to coat. Just before serving, stir in the marmalade.

"The hostess must be like the duck—calm and unruffled on the surface, and paddling like hell underneath."

—Anonymous

OVEN "FRENCH FRIES"

Here's a method for preparing "French Fries" that is super easy AND provides a safe and delectable treat for family and friends. Deep frying potatoes in shortening may taste good but they are often greasy and high in trans fat. Fast food French fries are worse, although some restaurants are beginning to switch to safer cooking oils.

Preheat oven to 450°

Ingredients

4 medium potatoes

3 tablespoons mild olive oil or canola

Sea salt to taste

Paprika

Procedure

Peel potatoes and cut lengthwise in strips, roughly ½ inch thick. Place on a baking sheet. Pour the oil over them and stir until well coated. Sprinkle with salt and dust with paprika. (Paprika adds flavor and acts as a browning agent.) Bake 30-40 minutes, stirring occasionally, until the "fries" are crisp and tender. Add more salt and paprika if needed.

Serves 4.

PECAN PILAF

This pilaf is full of flavor and texture with added crunch from the pecans. All this plus the fringe benefits of nuts and canola oil, both known to lower cholesterol.

Preheat oven to 325°

Ingredients

¾ cup pecans

2 ½ cups uncooked rice

¼ cup canola oil

5 cups chicken stock (homemade or substitute organic ready made broth)

1 teaspoon salt

Procedure

Spread the pecans on a cookie sheet and toast for 10-15 minutes. Remove from oven, coarsely chop, and set aside.

Heat oil in a large skillet, add the rice, and cook over low heat, stirring often, until the color of straw. Add the chicken stock, raise heat to high, and bring to a boil, stirring constantly. Lower heat, cover, and simmer 15 minutes or until rice is tender and stock is absorbed. Remove from heat and place a dish towel between the pan and the lid for 3 or 4 minutes to absorb any excess moisture. Fluff the rice with a fork and stir in the pecans.

Serves 8.

QUICK TOP of the STOVE BEANS and RICE

I was surprised to learn that beans and rice in combination form a complete protein. Here is the ideal dish for lowering cholesterol: quick and easy to prepare, no baking needed, and besides all that, delicious! Serve with a simple green salad, cold apple cider, and warm crusty bread. The perfect Saturday night supper.

Ingredients

½ cup rice

1 teaspoon canola oil

2 tablespoons olive oil

1 small onion, chopped

1 carrot, chopped small

2 cloves garlic, minced

1 can canned diced tomatoes with juice

2 tablespoon brown sugar

1 teaspoon vinegar

2 (11 ounce) cans baked beans

Procedure

Cook rice according to package directions, substituting canola oil for butter. Remove from heat and fluff with a folk. Set aside uncovered. In a large frying pan or heavy soup pot, sauté onion and carrots in olive oil until tender and the onions are transparent. Add garlic and cook for 1 minute more. Stir in tomatoes, sugar, and vinegar. Cook over medium low heat for 10 minutes. Open the can of beans and remove any small pieces of fatty pork that may be sitting on top. Discard pork. Add beans to pot. Stir in rice, cook 2 minutes or until heated through. Remove from heat and serve.

6-8 servings.

Jeannie Serpa

QUINOA TABOULI PLUS

This my version of Tabouli, sometimes spelled Tabbouli or Tabouleh. It is made with quinoa (pronounced keen-wah) in place of the traditional cracked wheat. The plus in its title refers to the addition of the garbanzo beans. They are high in protein and contain no harmful saturated fat, trans fat, or cholesterol.

Ingredients

1 cup water
½ cup quinoa, well rinsed
½ teaspoon salt
1 cup red or orange bell pepper, seeded and chopped
2 vine ripened tomatoes, chopped
1 cup canned garbanzo beans (chickpeas), rinsed in cold
  water and drained
½ cup chopped green onions (scallions)
2 tablespoons chopped fresh parsley
2 tablespoons chopped fresh mint, preferably peppermint
2 tablespoons fresh lemon juice
Sea salt
Freshly ground black pepper

Procedure

In a small saucepan, combine water, salt, and quinoa. Bring to a boil; reduce heat, cover, and simmer 15-20 minutes or until water is absorbed. Remove from heat, stir, set aside and allow to cool.

In a large bowl, combine bell pepper, tomatoes, garbanzo beans, scallions, parsley, and peppermint. Add lemon juice and toss lightly to mix. Add the cooled cooked quinoa, combining completely. Season to taste with salt and pepper. Cover and place in refrigerator for 2 to 4 hours. Makes 4-6 servings.

ROASTED BRUSSELS SPROUTS #1

Many people think they dislike these little green cabbages and I was a member of that club until I tried the following recipe. An important factor here is that they have more soluble fiber than any other vegetable. Remember, soluble fiber is a cholesterol fighter! The secret to great tasting Brussels sprouts? Do not overcook.

Preheat oven to 400°

Ingredients

1 pound Brussels sprouts

2 tablespoons extra virgin olive oil

1 tablespoon lemon juice

1 clove garlic, minced

Optional salt

Coarse ground black pepper

Procedure

Wash sprouts in cold water and remove tough outer leaves. Halve any large sprouts.

Drain and place on baking sheet. Drizzle on the olive oil and lemon juice, stir, be certain all sprouts are coated. Bake 15 minutes, stir, add garlic, and bake an additional 10-15 minutes or until tender crisp and slightly browned. Adjust seasonings and serve piping hot.

ROASTED BRUSSELS SPROUTS #2

Here's a recipe for Brussels sprouts that just may convert those who say they don't like them. When I first learned that Brussels sprouts contain more soluble fiber than any other vegetable, I was determined to develop a recipe that everyone would love. The secret to delicious sprouts? Never, ever overcook and season with a bit of zip.

Preheat oven to 400°

Ingredients

2 pounds Brussels sprouts

2 tablespoons extra virgin olive oil

1 teaspoon McCormick's Herb Garlic Seasoning

Red pepper flakes to taste

2 teaspoons grated Parmesan cheese (special treat)

Procedure

Wash sprouts in cold water, drain, remove tough outer leaves, and halve any oversized sprouts. Place on a cookie sheet, toss with oil and all seasonings *except cheese*. Roast 15 minutes, stir. Continue cooking 10-15 minutes more or until tender crisp and slightly browned. Do not overcook. Remove from oven, sprinkle with the Parmesan, then return to oven for *60 seconds only*. Except for fat free cheese, Parmesan is the safest cheese for those of us watching our cholesterol. Never overdo it and use very occasionally.

Serves 6.

Leftovers served cold on a bed of greens make a delicious salad.

ROSEMARY BAKED GARBANZOS

Not only are garbanzo beans known to lower cholesterol, just one half cup serving provides us with six whole grams of protein. Since this recipe includes a goodly portion of extra virgin olive oil, it is not only high in protein but also among the best dishes for lowering cholesterol. Olive oil is a monounsaturated (good) fat that effectively cuts LDL without altering HDL.

Preheat oven to 350°

Ingredients

3 large tomatoes

2 cans garbanzo beans (chickpeas)

1 large Vidalia or other sweet onion, chopped

1 clove garlic, minced

1 teaspoon dried rosemary

½ cup extra virgin olive oil

1 teaspoon salt

½ teaspoon coarse ground black pepper

Procedure

Blanch tomatoes by plunging into boiling water for one minute. Blanching helps to set color, preserve nutrients, and will render the tomatoes easy to peel. Remove skin, seed, and chop. Drain garbanzos and rinse in cold water. Combine both with onion, garlic, rosemary, olive oil, salt, and pepper in a casserole dish and bake for one hour. Adjust the seasonings.

Serves 6-7.

SAUTÉED GARBANZOS

Garbanzo beans and olive oil combine with herbs to produce a tasty, nutritious side dish that has cholesterol lowering effects. Serve these hot, cold, or at room temperature. Use leftovers as a topping for green salad or add to soup for additional flavor and protein.

Ingredients

2 peeled and crushed garlic cloves

3 tablespoons olive oil

2 cans garbanzo beans, drained, and rinsed in cold water

⅛ teaspoon dried oregano or ½ teaspoon chopped fresh

¼ teaspoon dried sweet basil or ¾ teaspoon

Salt

Red pepper flakes

Procedure

Sauté crushed garlic in olive oil over medium low heat for 2 or 3 minutes. Add garbanzos, oregano, basil, salt, and a few pepper flakes. Cook, stirring occasionally, until the beans are golden brown.

Serves 4-5.

SKILLET ZUCCHINI

This savory vegetable dish looks as though you've spent hours over a hot stove. Serve this hot, room temperature, or cold. It's just plain good and all the ingredients are cholesterol lowering.

Ingredients

2 tablespoons extra virgin olive oil

1 medium size onion or one large Vidalia onion, peeled and sliced thin

3 medium size zucchini, unpeeled, cut into ¼ inch thick slices

1 small bay leaf or ½ large

Coarse sea salt

Coarse black pepper

1 cup chopped tomatoes

A few flakes of dried red pepper (optional)

Procedure

In a large skillet, heat oil, add onion, and sauté over medium heat. Cook until transparent. Add zucchini, bay leaf, salt, and pepper. Cover and cook until tender crisp. Add tomatoes and red pepper. Continue to sauté covered until all vegetables are tender. Remove bay leaf. Transfer to a heated platter.

Serves 4-6.

SPICY GRILLED CORN ON THE COB

We all seem to love our sweet corn smothered in butter. (Not a good idea.) This is a bit unconventional, but absolutely delicious! Try it.

Ingredients

½ cup canola oil or mild olive oil

½ cup low fat mayonnaise

½ teaspoon cayenne pepper

¼ teaspoon salt

8 ears fresh corn, shucked

Procedure

Combine first 4 ingredients in a bowl. Spread about 1½ table-spoons of mixture on each ear of corn, and wrap each ear in heavy-duty aluminum foil.

Grill corn over high heat for about 20 minutes, turning frequently.

Serves 6-8.

Desserts

ANGEL FOOD VOLCANO CAKE (Quick and Easy)

Your saving grace! Free of saturated fat, trans fat, and cholesterol, here is the ideal dessert for those with high cholesterol. Whether store bought, made from a package mix, or "from scratch," in order to claim the name Angel Food Cake, egg whites (never yolks) must be used.

Ingredients

1 purchased Angel Food Cake

1 (6 ounce) container fat free, plain yogurt

8 ounce tub fat free Cool Whip*

1 (15 ounce) can crushed pineapple, completely drained

1 (11 ounce) can mandarin oranges, completely drained

Procedure

Combine yogurt and Cool Whip. Check to be sure the fruit is free of any juice. Fold the fruit into the yogurt mixture. Place the cake on a pretty platter and fill the center hole with the fruit combination, allowing the filling to spill over and cascade down the sides of the cake for a lava effect. Use dental floss, an electric knife, a serrated knife, or a cake divider for cutting angel food cake.

Serves 8-10.

Note: Remember to use Cool Whip for special treats only and always in moderation.

See Chapter 1: Safe Foods

CELESTIAL PUDDING CAKE

I almost named this dessert Flying Angel Pudding because it assembles so quickly. An impressive dish that will delight family and friends, this can be presented with pride at your most elegant dinner parties. And, keep in mind, Angel Food Cake is safe for those who are on "Cholesterol Watch."

Ingredients

¼ cup slivered almonds

1 Angel Food Cake (store bought or made from mix)

⅓ cup dry sherry

1 (11 ounce) can mandarin oranges

¼ cup toasted slivered almonds

1 (3 ¾ ounce) package Dream Whip

Procedure

Place almonds in a dry frying pan and "toast" over medium heat for 5-8 minutes or until golden and fragrant, stirring often.

Break cake into 1 inch chunks. Place chunks in an 8x12x2 inch baking dish. Drizzle sherry evenly over the cake. Drain oranges, reserving juice and ¼ cup of the oranges.

Spread remaining ¾ cup oranges over the cake. Sprinkle with almonds. Prepare Dream Whip following directions on package, substituting the reserved orange juice for the water. Distribute evenly over the cake. Chill for 2 hours. Just before serving, garnish with reserved oranges and mint leaves.

Serves 6-8.

DECADENT ANGELS

Since Angel Food Cake is made with the whites of eggs only, it is free of cholesterol. It contains no saturated fat nor trans fat either, making it the ideal cake for those of us on Cholesterol Watch. This is a rich, special occasion dessert. Use cocoa here in place of chocolate. Cocoa has no cholesterol and no saturated fat, while chocolate contains both.

Ingredients

Angel Food Cake (store bought, made from a mix or home-made)

Chocolate Icing #2

1 (8 ounce) tub fat free Cool Whip*

1 tablespoon cocoa

1 jar maraschino cherries, drained

Procedure

Cut cake into slices about 1 to 1 ½ inches thick. Distribute the slices on a cookie sheet that has been covered with parchment or waxed paper. Meanwhile, make the icing. Pour icing over the slices. Place on a wire rack and let the icing "set." (This is a little messy—I use tongs.) Combine Cool Whip with the cocoa, mixing thoroughly. Just before serving, place the iced slices on individual dessert plates and spoon on a dollop of the chocolate Cool Whip. Top each with a cherry. Oh, my!

cont...

CHOCOLATE ICING #2

Ingredients

1 cup powdered sugar

1 tablespoon cocoa

¼ cup fat free half & half cream

¼ teaspoon vanilla

Procedure

Place sugar, cocoa, and cream in a saucepan. Warm over medium heat, stirring constantly until sugar is dissolved. Turn up heat and bring rapidly to a boil. Boil for 2 minutes or until icing forms a thread when allowed to drip from a spoon. Immediately remove from heat and add vanilla. You want the icing to be just thin enough to pour over the cake. If too thick, add a little water.

*Note: Remember to use Cool Whip for special treats only and always in moderation.

See Chapter 1: Safe Foods

FROSTED CHOCOLATE CHERRY CUPCAKES

These cupcakes not only look great and taste great but they contain ingredients that have been proven to actually reduce cholesterol: oat bran, canola, and nuts. By using cocoa rather than chocolate you are safe, since cocoa has 0 cholesterol, 0 trans fat, and 0 saturated fat. Chocolate is high in all three. So celebrate and enjoy!

Preheat oven to 400°

Ingredients

1 cup oat bran hot cereal

1 ¼ cups presifted flour

¼ cup baking cocoa

1 tablespoon baking powder

1 teaspoon baking soda

½ cup brown sugar

1 cup fat free evaporated milk

4 ounces egg substitute or 3 egg whites

3 tablespoons canola oil

1 teaspoon vanilla

½ cup drained and chopped maraschino cherries

Procedure

Combine the oat bran, flour, cocoa, baking powder, baking soda, and sugar, mixing well. Stir in the milk, egg substitute or whites, oil, and vanilla. Combine well. Gently fold in the cherries. Spray cupcake tin with canola cooking spray and dust with flour or line with foil cups. Spoon batter into cupcake chambers until almost full. Bake 15 minutes or until a toothpick inserted in the center comes out clean. Cool about 10 minutes before removing from pan. Cool completely before frosting with Chocolate Icing #3.

CHOCOLATE ICING #3

Ingredients

2 cups powdered (confectionary) sugar
4 teaspoons cocoa
Water to mix
Walnuts or pecan halves for garnish

Procedure

Sift sugar and cocoa together. Gradually stir in enough water to form a stiff icing. Frost each cupcake and garnish with a walnut or pecan half.

Yield: 15 cupcakes.

GRILLED BANANAS
with MOCK CRÈME FRAÎCHE

Surprise family and guests with this delectable dessert that's a bit out of the ordinary. This one is not only cholesterol friendly, it's full of antioxidants and potassium. I must advise readers not to overdo fat free products. Check nutrition labels. What is being used for flavor to take the place of saturated fat? Large amounts of salt? Corn syrup?

Ingredients

4 bananas, unpeeled and washed
3 ounces fat free sour cream
3 ounces fat free Cool Whip*
Cinnamon

cont...

Sliced fresh strawberries

Mint leaves for garnish

Procedure

Grill bananas until brown and hot inside (about 5 minutes each side).

Meanwhile, make the mock crème fraîche by combining sour cream and Cool Whip. The crème fraîche that is available in the dairy section of your supermarket is high in cholesterol and saturated fat.

Remove bananas from grill, slice the skin lengthwise, and remove the fruit. Place bananas on individual dessert plates. Spoon on the crème fraîche and sprinkle with cinnamon. Scatter strawberries over all and garnish with mint leaves. Present while hot.

Serves 4.

*Note: Remember to use Cool Whip for special treats only and always in moderation.

See Chapter 1: Safe Foods

ICE CREAM PIE with PEANUTTY CRUST and SHAVED CHOCOLATE

Kids, both big and little, love this pie!

Ingredients

1 ¼ cups store bought graham cracker crumbs

¼ cup sugar

5 tablespoons melted soft tub margarine, low in saturated fat and with 0 trans fat

1 teaspoon cinnamon

cont...

½ gallon non fat vanilla frozen yogurt*

¼ cup finely chopped dry roasted peanuts

2 tablespoons coarsely chopped peanuts

8 ounce container fat free Cool Whip**

½ bar of dark chocolate (70% cacao), frozen

Not to be confused with regular yogurt. Frozen yogurt resembles ice cream and can be found in ice cream shops and in the ice cream department of your supermarket. Kemps is an excellent brand and is very close to real ice cream in taste and in texture.

Procedure

Mix cracker crumbs, sugar, melted margarine, cinnamon, and peanuts together. When measuring crumbs, pack loosely in a measuring cup and level off with a knife. Use a large spoon to press the mixture into the bottom and up the side of a 9 inch pie pan.

Freeze the shell for 10 minutes before filling.

Meanwhile, allow the frozen yogurt to soften until easy to spread but not soupy. Remove shell from freezer and spoon in the softened yogurt, mounding it high in the center. Scatter the chopped peanuts over the top. Spread with Cool Whip and return to freezer until set.

Just before serving, dip the bottom of the pie pan in hot water. This makes for easier removal. Remove the chocolate bar from the freezer and use a vegetable peeler to shave decorative chocolate curls over the top of the Cool Whip. (Frozen chocolate is much easier to shave.)

This makes a large pie and will yield 10-12 servings.

**Note: Remember to use Cool Whip for special treats only and always in moderation.*

See Chapter 1: Safe Foods

LEMON BLUEBERRY CRANBERRY TEACAKES

It's teatime! Almost everyone loves the flavor of blueberries with lemon. Add Craisins (dried sweetened cranberries) and you have a refreshing, fruity teacake that is perfect for an afternoon break. These are moist and full of antioxidants, and the canola oil, cinnamon, and oat bran supply cholesterol lowering benefits.

Preheat oven to 400°

Ingredients

2 ½ cups oat bran hot cereal, uncooked

1 tablespoon baking powder

1 teaspoon baking soda

1 tablespoon pumpkin spice

1 teaspoon salt (optional)

1 cup skim milk or fat free evaporated milk

4 tablespoons canola oil

3 egg whites (extra large)

2 ounces (⅓ of a 6 ounce container) fat free or reduced fat lemon yogurt

1 tablespoon freshly squeezed lemon juice

½ cup Craisins

1 cup fresh blueberries

Canola baking spray

Procedure

Mix oat bran, baking powder, baking soda, pumpkin spice, and salt until well combined. Add milk, oil, egg whites, yogurt, and lemon juice. Gently fold in the Craisins. Set aside for 5 minutes

cont...

(the batter will thicken on standing). Meanwhile, generously spray a cupcake pan. Gently fold the blueberries into the batter. Next, spoon batter into prepared pan, almost filling each chamber. Bake on middle rack of oven for 12 to 15 minutes, being careful not to overbake. Let stand 5 minutes before removing from pan. Serve warm or store completely cooled cakes in an air tight container in refrigerator or freezer. Warm frozen cakes in microwave for 30 to 35 seconds. Since microwaves vary, test first. Refrigerated cakes may require only 15 to 20 seconds in microwave or simply bring them to room temperature before serving.

Yield: 10 to 12 teacakes.

"LET THEM EAT CAKE" CAKE

It is said that centuries ago Marie Antoinette, when told her subjects were starving and had no bread, replied, "Let them eat cake." Keep in mind that Angel Food Cake has 0 cholesterol, 0 saturated fat, and 0 trans fat. This is the safest, possibly the only cake, that can boast that claim. So I say, "Let us eat cake." Indulge and enjoy!

Ingredients

1 store bought Angel Food Cake (or make from a mix)
½ cup fat free Cool Whip* (or fat free Dream Whip, mixed)
¼ cup seedless raspberry jam
Chocolate Icing #1

cont...

Procedure

Place strips of wax paper around the edges of a cake plate. Position them so they can be removed after your cake has been iced, thus preventing those messy icing "drips." Cut the cake into three even layers. Center the largest layer on the plate and cover it with jam. Top this with the second largest layer and spread with Cool Whip, holding in place for a moment or two to be certain this layer does not slide. If it does, remove some of the Cool Whip. Finally, add the third layer. Frost with Chocolate Icing #1.

CHOCOLATE ICING #1

Ingredients

2 cup confectionary (powdered) sugar
4 teaspoon cocoa
Water

Procedure

Sift sugar and cocoa together into a bowl. Stir in enough water to form a smooth, easy-to-spread icing.

Note: Remember to use Cool Whip for special treats only and always in moderation.

See Chapter 1: Safe Foods

MANGO SORBET CREAM PIE

Preheat oven to 350°

Ingredients

1 ¼ cups store bought graham cracker crumbs

¼ cup granulated sugar

5 tablespoons soft tub margarine, melted

2 quarts Häagen Dazs mango sorbet

¼ cup sliced almonds

8 ounce container fat free Cool Whip*

1 fresh ripe mango, peeled and diced

Procedure

Measure graham cracker crumbs carefully, spooning loosely into measuring cup and leveling off with a knife. Combine crumbs with sugar and melted margarine. Use the back of a large spoon to press the mixture into the bottom and up the side of a 9 inch pie pan. Bake for 5 to 10 minutes, cool completely, and place in freezer for 10 minutes.

Allow the sorbet to soften until easy to spread yet not "soupy."

Meanwhile, in a dry skillet over medium heat, toast the almonds until golden and fragrant (5-10 minutes). Remove from heat and set aside to cool. Remove crust from freezer and spoon in the sorbet, mounding it up in the center. Return to freezer and allow sorbet to freeze until firm.

Stir the almonds into the Cool Whip, remove the pie from the freezer, and add a layer of diced mangoes. Pile on the Cool Whip mixture and return to freezer until almost ready to serve. Let the pie sit at room temperature for 5 minutes before cutting.

cont...

This is a "mile high" pie and will serve 10 to 12.

*Note: Remember to use Cool Whip for special treats only and always in moderation.

See Chapter 1: Safe Foods

MANGO SWIRL

Easy as 1-2-3!

Ready for a legal treat? This food plan is not all about sacrifice. It is wise to reward yourself on a regular basis and there is certainly no need to feel deprived. Try this delicious, satisfying desert.

Ingredients

1 cup fat free mango sorbet (Häagen Dazs)
½ cup no fat plain yogurt
½ fat free Cool Whip
½ cup large-dice mango

Procedure

Allow the sorbet to soften slightly while you prepare the mango. Combine the yogurt and Cool Whip. Add sorbet and swirl just a bit. Top with mango.

Variations

Substitute raspberry sorbet with fresh or frozen raspberries or strawberry sorbet with fresh or frozen strawberries.

*Note: Remember to use Cool Whip for special treats only and always in moderation.

See Chapter 1: Safe Foods

MY MOTHER'S STRAWBERRY SHORTCAKE

If my mom were living today she would be 103 years young. It wasn't often that she took short cuts with her cooking, but this one is the exception. I'm typing this from her original handwritten copy, which is yellowed with age and stained with red Jell-O. Little did she know she was making a low cholesterol dessert to be published years later by her daughter. Thank you, Mom.

Ingredients

3 (3 ounce) packages Strawberry Jell-O

1 pound frozen sliced strawberries

1 purchased Angel Food Cake, plain or strawberry flavored

1 (8 ounce) container fat free Cool Whip*

Whole fresh strawberries for garnish (optional)

Procedure

Place dry Jell-O in a bowl and add 3 cups boiling water, stirring until Jell-O is dissolved.

Add the frozen strawberries and stir until berries are thawed. Allow to cool.

Break the cake into chunks and distribute evenly in the bottom of a 9x13x2 inch baking dish. Pour the Jell-O mixture over the cake. Let cool and refrigerate until firm. Just before serving, spread Cool Whip over the top. (Mom used heavy cream whipped, a no-no for those of us on cholesterol watch.) Garnish with fresh strawberries. This is so good, so easy, and so cholesterol friendly!

Serves 10-12.

Mary Lillian Carroll

NOT to be TRIFLED WITH TRIFLE

Trifle dishes are large, round, straight-sided clear glass containers, designed especially to show off this stunning dessert. If you don't have one, use any large clear glass container. Free of harmful fat and cholesterol, this sumptuous dessert is safe for cholesterol watchers and makes for a stunning presentation. The rum version is for adults only, of course. You might vary this trifle by substituting raspberry jam and fresh raspberries or mandarin oranges and orange marmalade.

Ingredients

One Angel Food Cake, ready made or made from a package mix

Strawberry jam

¼ cup white rum or orange juice

1 (8 ounce) tub fat free Cool Whip*

1 pint fresh strawberries, hulled and halved

A few mint leaves (optional)

Procedure

Cut cake into one inch cubes (roughly). Spread each piece with a thin coat of jam. Pile the pieces into a trifle bowl. While tossing gently, very slowly (almost drop by drop) pour the orange juice or white rum over all. (Dark rum will ruin the lovely color.) Carefully fold in the Cool Whip, then just as carefully fold in the strawberries. Garnish with a cluster of mint leaves in the center and wow your guests.

Note: Remember to use Cool Whip for special treats only and always in moderation.

See Chapter 1: Safe Foods

POACHED PEARS with RASPBERRY SAUCE

Ingredients

6 pears, unpeeled
¼ cup lemon juice
4 cups water

Procedure

Cut a slice off the bottom of each pear so that they will stand upright. Place them in a large saucepan. Add water and lemon juice. Bring to a boil, reduce heat, and simmer for 15-20 minutes. Pears should be soft, yet firm enough to hold together. Remove from liquid, drain, and place in a baking dish. Refrigerate for several hours. When ready to present, place each pear in an individual serving dish with raspberry sauce poured over. Serve with dessert fork and knife.

"Eating is one of the great pleasures in life and, for many, cooking is another. To enjoy cooking a great meal is beyond words."

—Normand Leclair

RASPBERRY SAUCE

Ingredients

1 jar seedless raspberry jam, all fruit, no sugar

3 tablespoons orange juice

2 tablespoons lime juice

2 tablespoons water

Procedure

Combine jam, orange juice, lime juice, and water in a saucepan. Warm over medium heat, stirring constantly, adding more water if needed. Serve warm or at room temperature. Cooled sauce can be refrigerated and used cold or reheated.

"Spaghetti can be eaten most successfully if you inhale it like a vacuum cleaner."

—Sophia Loren

RASPBERRY PARFAIT

A light dessert that is just plain pretty and nutritious in many ways. We know that honey is good for us. This recipe also provides antioxidants and vitamin C from the strawberries and orange juice. In addition to all that, it is cholesterol friendly.

Ingredients

4 cups fresh raspberries

½ cup orange juice

1 tablespoon honey

1 cup fat free Cool Whip

1 cup fat free plain yogurt

Mint leaves for garnish

Procedure

Combine raspberries, orange juice, and honey in a food processor and process until smooth. Pour into a 1 ½ quart casserole dish. Cover and freeze until slushy (about 20-30 minutes). Return mixture to food processor and process again until smooth. Freeze until firm (about an hour). Mix the Cool Whip and yogurt together. To serve, spoon into parfait glasses or any stemmed dessert dishes. Alternate the raspberry mixture with the yogurt mixture, ending with the yogurt. Garnish each with a mint leaf.

Serves 6-8.

*Note: Remember to use Cool Whip for special treats only and always in moderation.

See Chapter 1: Safe Foods

RUBY BANANAS

Here we have a delicious contrast between hot and cold, sweet and tart. In addition, this scrumptious and delightfully different dessert is the perfect "company" dish. The cranberry sauce is free of saturated fat, trans fat, and cholesterol. Bananas are high in potassium and walnuts are rich in omega-3, one of the warriors against high cholesterol.

Preheat oven to 250°

Ingredients

6 bananas

1 (16 ounce) can whole cranberry sauce

1 tablespoon fresh lemon juice

1 teaspoon cinnamon

8 ounce container of fat free Cool Whip*

½ cup walnut pieces

Procedure

Slice bananas lengthwise, then crosswise. Arrange a single layer of bananas in a 9x13 inch baking dish. Sprinkle with lemon juice.

Place cranberry sauce in a bowl and mash with a potato masher. Stir in cinnamon. Spread the cranberry mixture over the bananas and heat in oven for 20 minutes. Place in individual dishes while warm and top each with a dollop of Cool Whip. Scatter walnut pieces over all and serve with pride!

Serves 6.

Note: Remember to use Cool Whip for special treats only and always in moderation.

See Chapter 1: Safe Foods

Jeannie Serpa

STRAWBERRY ICE CREAM PIE

This is equally delicious made with raspberry frozen yogurt and frozen raspberries, thawed. Treat yourself, your family, and guests to a dessert that's cool, refreshing, and sweet. An impressive dessert, so easy to prepare. Even more perfect when berries are in season.

Preheat oven to 350°

Ingredients

1 ¼ cups store bought graham cracker crumbs

¼ cup granulated sugar

5 tablespoons soft tub margarine, melted

1 quart fat free frozen strawberry yogurt*

1 pint fresh strawberries, hulled and sliced or frozen sliced berries, thawed

6 ounces (¾ of an 8 ounce container) fat free Cool Whip**

8 whole strawberries for garnish

* Not to be confused with regular yogurt. Frozen yogurt resembles ice cream and can be found in ice cream shops and the ice cream department of your supermarket. Kemps is an excellent brand and is very close to real ice cream in taste and texture.

Procedure

Measure graham cracker crumbs carefully, spooning loosely into measuring cup and leveling off with a knife. Combine crumbs with sugar and melted margarine. Using the back of a large spoon, press the mixture into the bottom and up the side of a 9 inch pie pan. Bake for 5-10 minutes, cool completely, and place in freezer for 10 minutes before filling.

cont...

Meanwhile, soften the frozen yogurt until workable but not soupy. Remove pie shell from the freezer, spoon in the frozen yogurt, spread evenly, and return to freezer until firm. For easier serving, dip bottom of the pie plate into hot water. Serve topped with sliced strawberries and 2 tablespoons Cool Whip. Garnish with whole strawberries.

Serves 8.

**Note: Remember to use Cool Whip for special treats only and always in moderation.*

See Chapter 1: Safe Foods

"I shall content myself with merely declaring my conviction that, for the seeker who would live in the fear of God and would see him face to face, restraint in diet both as to quantity and quality is as essential as restraint in thought and speech."

—Mahatma Gandhi

STRAWBERRY PARFAIT

This is oh, so pretty! Cool, light, refreshing, and safe for us cholesterol watchers. Everyone will love this whether they are cholesterol conscious or not. For anyone who doesn't care for plain yogurt, the magic combination of yogurt and Cool Whip wins them over. Of course, you can use plain Cool Whip if you prefer, but give this a try.

Ingredients

4 cups fresh strawberries

½ cup pineapple juice

¼ cup honey

1 (6 ounce) container fat free plain yogurt

1 (8 ounce) carton fat free Cool Whip*

6 fresh strawberries for garnish

Procedure

Combine strawberries, pineapple juice, and honey in a food processor and blend until smooth. Pour into a 1 ½ quart casserole dish. Cover and freeze until slushy, about 20-30 minutes. Return mixture to food processor and process until smooth. Freeze until firm (at least one hour). Meanwhile, combine yogurt and Cool Whip. Refrigerate.

To serve: scoop small amounts the frozen mixture into parfait dishes or any stemmed dessert dishes, then a small amount of the yogurt mix, then more of the frozen mix. Alternate the layers, ending with the yogurt mix. Garnish with a fresh strawberry and serve immediately. Yummy!

Serves 6.

Note: Remember to use Cool Whip for special treats only and always in moderation.

See Chapter 1: Safe Foods

STRAWBERRY PEACH PARFAIT

Bet you thought you would be foregoing parfaits while on this choles-terol diet. Well, surprise, surprise! This delectable dessert is guaranteed to satisfy. It is a beautiful to look at and yummy.

Ingredients

4 large fresh peaches
3- 6 ounce containers fat free peach yogurt
12 fresh strawberries, sliced
Mint leaves for garnish
¼ cup chopped walnuts

Procedure

Peel peaches, remove stones, and slice. Layer yogurt, peaches, and strawberries in parfait glasses or stemware, ending with the yogurt. Scatter walnuts on top and garnish with a mint leaf.

Serves 5-6.

"Food is our common ground, a universal experience."

—James Beard

TRICIA'S APPLE CAKE

Canola oil, cinnamon, and walnuts are among the leaders in the battle against cholesterol. What a delicious way to help win that battle! Most cakes are on the no-no list for any one with high cholesterol, since most are made with butter, eggs, and high fat icings. Tricia's savory cake will stand on its own, needing no icing whatsoever. You may be tempted to peel the apples, but trust me—there is no need!

Preheat oven to 350°

Ingredients

1 ¾ cups sugar

4 ounces egg substitute

1 ¼ cups canola oil

3 cups flour

1 teaspoon baking soda

½ teaspoon salt

2 teaspoons cinnamon

2 teaspoons vanilla

½ cup chopped walnuts

3 cups chopped *unpeeled* apples

Procedure

Combine sugar, egg substitute, and oil in a large bowl. Sift together the flour, baking soda, salt, and cinnamon. Add to the sugar mixture, combining well. Incorporate vanilla, nuts, and apples, mixing just enough to moisten. Spread in an ungreased 9x13 inch baking pan or dish. Bake 45-60 minutes. Allow to cool and cut in squares.

Tricia Evangelista

Cookies

&

Candies

ADULTS ONLY CANDY BALLS

Since these candies are not cooked, the alcohol will not evaporate. It is therefore extremely important that these be served at gatherings where there are no children or alcoholics present.

Ingredients

1 cup powered sugar

2 tablespoons baker's cocoa

½ cup bourbon

2 tablespoons light corn syrup

2 ½ cups crushed vanilla wafers

1 cup pecan pieces

½ cup powdered sugar

Procedure

Sift sugar and cocoa together. Combine corn syrup and bourbon, then stir into the sugar mixture. Add and thoroughly mix in the vanilla wafers and pecans. Roll the dough into small balls and dredge in powdered sugar.

"Eat breakfast like a king, lunch like a prince, and dinner like a pauper."

—Adelle Davis

BANANA OATMEAL COOKIES

In addition to being extremely good for your cholesterol, these cookies (because they are sugar free) have the fringe benefit of being very low in calories. The bananas and raisins provide natural sweetness. Each cookie has only about 45 calories!

Preheat oven to 350°

Ingredients

3 bananas, mashed

3 cups uncooked quick cooking oatmeal

½ cup raisins

1 teaspoon cinnamon

¼ teaspoon nutmeg

⅓ cup soft tub margarine, melted

¼ cup skim milk

1 teaspoon vanilla

Procedure

Thoroughly combine all ingredients, stirring well. Let stand for 5 minutes, allowing the oatmeal to absorb moisture. Drop by heaping teaspoonfuls onto 2 ungreased cookie sheets and bake for 15 to 20 minutes. An alternative method is to roll the dough into ping pong ball size balls, place on cookie sheets, and flatten slightly with a spoon. Proceed to bake for 15 to 20 minutes. Whichever method you use, let the cookies remain on the cookie sheets for 5 minutes before removing. Transfer to a wire rack and allow cool completely.

CANDIED WALNUTS

Walnuts have been proven to help lower cholesterol. They are also a source of protein, antioxidants, and omega-3 fatty acid.

Preheat oven to 350°

Ingredients

3 cups raw walnuts
1 quart water
2 cups sugar
¼ cup water
Sea salt

Procedure

Carefully drop walnuts into one quart of boiling water and boil for five minutes. Drain in a sieve. Rinse briefly in cold water.

Add sugar and ¼ cup of water to a saucepan and bring to a boil. Add the walnuts, stirring until all the liquid disappears.

Line a cookie sheet with parchment paper or foil. Spread the nuts evenly and bake for 7-8 minutes. Stir and bake an additional 7-8 minutes. Remove from oven and immediately sprinkle with sea salt.

Makes 3 cups.

CHOCOLATE HAZELNUT MACAROONS

Preheat oven to 325°

Ingredients

½ cup hazelnuts

¾ cup quick oats

2 tablespoons flour

⅓ cup brown sugar

6 tablespoons cocoa powder, unsweetened

4 egg whites at room temperature

1 teaspoon pure vanilla

½ teaspoon salt

⅓ cup plus 1 tablespoon granulated sugar

Procedure

Place hazelnuts in a dry skillet over medium heat. Toast until golden brown. Transfer nuts to a dish towel, fold towel over the nuts, and rub vigorously, removing as much as you can of the skins. Using a nut chopper or food processor, finely chop the nuts. Combine nuts, oats, flour, brown sugar, and cocoa powder. Set aside.

Use an electric mixer to beat the egg whites, vanilla, and salt on high until soft peaks form. Gradually add the granulated sugar, continuing to beat on high, until stiff peaks form. Gently and carefully fold in the hazelnut mixture. Place a sheet of parchment paper on a cookie sheet and spoon level tablespoons of the dough onto the parchment. Bake until tops of cookies no longer appear wet. About 15-17 minutes. Remove to a cooling rack. Completely cooled cookies may be stored loosely in an airtight container.

Yield: 36 cookies.

CHOCOLATE NO BAKE OATMEAL COOKIES

Do you have a "sweet tooth"? These are sure to satisfy. Munch on them at room temperature, chilled, or as I like them, straight from the freezer. They are made with cocoa rather than chocolate. If you are a chocoholic, you'll be pleased to know that although chocolate contains saturated fat, cocoa does not! These have the added cholesterol lowering benefits of peanut butter, oatmeal, and nuts.

Ingredients

½ cup soft margarine

½ cup skim milk or fat free evaporated milk

1 ½ cups sugar

⅓ cup cocoa

3 tablespoons peanut butter

1 teaspoon vanilla

3 cups oatmeal (regular or quick)

½ cup raisins

½ cup chopped pecans

Procedure

In a saucepan, combine margarine, milk, sugar, and cocoa. Boil for 3 minutes, stirring occasionally. Remove from heat and add peanut butter, stirring until melted. Next add vanilla, oatmeal, raisins, and nuts, mixing until well combined. Allow to cool slightly. Meanwhile, cover a cookie sheet with wax or parchment paper. Drop by the teaspoonful onto the paper. For neater looking round cookies, rub palms of both hands with canola oil and roll a teaspoonful of dough into a ball. (The oil will keep the dough from sticking to your fingers.) Place the balls on the waxed or parchment paper, leave as is, or flatten each by pressing down with a spoon. Proceed as above. When completely

cont...

cooled, put in a covered container. Refrigerate or freeze.

Makes 30-36 cookies

GLAZED PECANS

Preheat oven to 250°

Ingredients

1 egg white
½ teaspoon cinnamon
½ teaspoon salt
1 tablespoon orange juice
½ cup sugar
3 cups pecan halves
Canola baking spray

Procedure

Separate the egg, being careful not to get any yolk into the white. Beat with a fork until foamy. Add cinnamon, salt, and orange juice. Fold in the sugar and combine well. Add pecans. Generously coat a cookie sheet with canola spray, spread pecans evenly, and bake for 45-60 minutes. Turn every 15 minutes. Cool completely and store in an airtight container.

MICROWAVE PEPPERMINT CANDY BRITTLE

Complicated candy recipes involving syrups and special candy thermometers are not for me. My grandchildren love these and prefer them to the traditional peanut brittle.

Ingredients

Canola baking spray or canola oil

½ cup light corn syrup

1 cup sugar

1 cup crushed hard peppermint candies or peppermint candy canes

1 teaspoon soft tub margarine

1 teaspoon vanilla

1 teaspoon baking soda

Procedure

Lightly coat a baking sheet with canola and set aside. Combine corn syrup and sugar in a 1 ½ quart microwave safe dish. Mix until well blended. Microwave on high for 4 minutes. Stir, return to microwave, and cook an additional 4-5 minutes on high or until the mixture is light brown in color. Stir in margarine and vanilla, blending well. Again on high, microwave another 1-2 minutes. Now add the baking soda and stir gently until foamy. Quickly pour onto the baking sheet and spread evenly. Sprinkle candy over the surface and press lightly while hot. Allow to cool completely before breaking into pieces.

Yield: about 2 pounds.

NO COOK PEANUT BUTTER BALLS

Quick and easy. Both peanut butter and pecans have been proven to help reduce cholesterol levels.

Ingredients

1 cup smooth peanut butter at room temperature
1 cup light corn syrup
1 ¼ cups powdered milk
½ cup pecans, chopped

Procedure

Mix together peanut butter, corn syrup, and powdered milk. Fold in pecans. Roll into balls about ½ to ¾ inches in diameter. That's it!

OAT BRAN CONGO SQUARES

Years ago, my sister Nancy shared with me her recipe for Congo Squares. They have since become a family tradition. No holiday or family gathering was complete without these delectable treats that were high in both saturated fat and cholesterol. I have taken Nancy's recipe and converted it to a cholesterol lowering version that not only meets with her approval, but is proving to be as popular as the original. To date, I haven't served these oat bran chocolate chip bars to anyone who hasn't loved them. Try these. They are mouth watering! If your cholesterol level is under control, you may wish to use real eggs in place of egg substitute, especially since the eggs will be distributed among 72 squares. Semi-sweet chocolate contains some saturated fat, so don't over indulge on these.

cont...

Preheat oven to 350°

Ingredients

1 (14 ounce) box brown sugar (I use one package of Brownulated Sugar. It pours easily and does not harden.)

⅔ cup canola oil

6 ounces egg substitute or 3 eggs

1 teaspoon vanilla

1 tablespoon fresh lemon juice

1 cup oat bran

1 ¾ cups presifted flour

2 ½ teaspoons baking powder

½ teaspoon salt

1 (12 ounce package) semi-sweet chocolate chips

Canola cooking spray or soft tub margarine

Procedure

In a large mixing bowl, combine thoroughly the sugar, canola oil, egg substitute, vanilla, and lemon juice. Stir in the oat bran and incorporate well. Add the flour, baking powder, salt, and mix well. (Batter will be thick.) Finally, stir in the chocolate chips.

Generously coat both bottom and sides of a 9x13 inch baking dish (or two 8x8 inch brownie pans) with canola oil, cooking spray, or soft margarine. Spoon in the batter, spreading so that the batter around the edges is thicker than in the center. This will prevent a too crusty edge. Bake 22-25 minutes. Do not overbake.

Allow to cool completely and cut into squares. These freeze well and make great gifts. (Your friends will love you!)

Makes 72 squares.

PEPPERMINT MERINGUES

These are light with a refreshing hint of mint and good for your cholesterol. For pink mint meringues, substitute a little red food coloring for the green. Bake meringues on dry days. They are affected by high humidity.

Preheat oven to 200°

Ingredients

4 egg whites at room temperature

½ teaspoon cream of tartar

¾ cup granulated sugar

½ teaspoon peppermint extract

Green food coloring

2 finely crushed hard peppermint candies

Procedure

Line 2 cookie sheets with foil. Eggs should be at room temperature. Separate eggs with care, being sure that no yolk gets into the whites. Place in a glass or stainless steel bowl and add cream of tartar. Beat on high speed until the whites are foamy. While still beating, gradually add the sugar until the mixture is thick and stiff peaks form. Add peppermint extract and food coloring. Transfer to a pastry bag with a large round tip and squeeze small amounts of batter onto cookie sheets, about 26 per sheet. No pastry bag? Not a problem. Substitute a resealable plastic bag and cut ½ inch off a corner. Sprinkle each meringue with just a little of the crushed candy. Bake for 2 hours at this low temperature. Turn off oven. Let the meringues remain in the oven for 30 minutes. Remove and allow to cool completely. Store in air tight containers. Do not freeze.

Yield 4 ½ dozen.

POPCORN CANDY BALLS

Ingredients

⅔ cups granulated sugar

½ cup water

2 ½ tablespoons light corn syrup

⅛ teaspoon salt

⅓ teaspoon vinegar

Canola oil

6 cups popcorn

Procedure

In a saucepan, combine sugar, water, corn syrup, salt, and vinegar. Stir until the sugar is dissolved. Place over medium high heat and bring to a boil. Reduce heat, cover, and cook for roughly 3 minutes or until steam washes down the sides of the pan. Uncover and continue cooking *without stirring,* nearly to a hard crack stage. If you have a candy thermometer, this will register about 290°. Remove from heat and immediately pour over the popcorn. Toss gently with a wooden spoon until well coated. When cool enough to handle, lightly coat fingers with canola oil and press into balls.

PUMPKIN- OATMEAL RAISIN COOKIES

Enjoy these scrumptious cookies and have the comfort of knowing they are good for you! Oatmeal, cinnamon, and walnuts have been proven to lower cholesterol. Walnuts are high in omega-3 fat and among our greatest allies. Pumpkin (rich in vitamin A) and raisins have O cholesterol, O saturated fat, and O trans fat.

cont...

Preheat oven to 350°

Ingredients

2 cups all-purpose flour

1 ⅓ cups quick or old-fashioned oats

1 teaspoon baking soda

1 teaspoon ground cinnamon

½ teaspoon salt

1 cup soft tub margarine

1 cup packed brown sugar

1 cup granulated sugar

1 cup canned pumpkin

2 ounces egg substitute

1 teaspoon vanilla extract

1 cup chopped walnuts

1 cup raisins

Canola cooking spray

Procedure

Combine flour, oats, baking soda, cinnamon, and salt in medium bowl. Beat margarine, brown sugar, and granulated sugar in a large bowl until light and fluffy. Add pumpkin, egg substitute, vanilla, and mix well. Add flour mixture to the pumpkin mixture; mix well. Stir in nuts and raisins. Drop by rounded tablespoon onto 2 canola sprayed baking sheets. Bake 14 to 16 minutes or until cookies are lightly browned and set in their centers. Cool on baking sheets 2-5 minutes; remove to wire racks to cool completely.

Makes about 4 dozen cookies.

PUMPKIN PECAN BARS

These will help lower cholesterol and please the palate. Who says you need to suffer in order to lower your cholesterol? They smell so good you will be tempted to eat them hot!

Preheat oven to 350°

Ingredients

½ cup old fashioned or quick oats

1 cup flour

½ cup brown sugar

½ cup soft tub margarine (never stick margarine!)

¾ cup granulated sugar

1 can pumpkin

2 teaspoons cinnamon

½ teaspoon nutmeg

¼ teaspoon ginger

4 ounces egg substitute or 3 egg whites

1 can fat free evaporated milk

½ cup chopped pecans

¼ cup brown sugar

Procedure

In a small bowl, thoroughly mix oats, flour, brown sugar, and margarine until crumbly.

Press into bottom of a 9x13 inch baking pan. Bake 15 minutes.

Thoroughly combine granulated sugar, pumpkin, cinnamon, nutmeg, and ginger in a large bowl. Incorporate the milk and eggs and mix well.

cont...

Pour over the pre-baked crust, distributing evenly. Bake 20 minutes.

In a small bowl, combine pecans and brown sugar and sprinkle over the filling. Resume baking 15 to 20 minutes or until a knife inserted in the center comes out clean. Leave in pan until completely cool. Cut into squares and serve proudly.

Yield: 12 bars

Note: Remember to use Cool Whip for special treats only and always in moderation.

See Chapter 1: Safe Foods

"*Tell me what you eat and I'll tell you what you are.*"

—Anthelme Brillat-Savarin

SIMPLE MERINGUES

Never attempt to make meringues when the humidity is high. These old time confections are always popular and since they are made with egg whites and no fat, they are good for us cholesterol watchers.

Preheat oven to 225°

Ingredients

4 egg whites
1 teaspoon vanilla
⅛ teaspoon cream of tartar
1 cup powdered sugar
½ teaspoon cinnamon

Procedure

Eggs should be at room temperature before separating. Be careful not to get even slightest bit of yolk into the whites. It is important to beat egg whites in a glass or stainless steel bowl. Beat until foamy with an electric mixer. Add vanilla and cream of tartar. Sift the powdered sugar and cinnamon together, then add one tablespoon at a time to the egg whites, while continuing to beat. Beat until the mixture forms stiff peaks on the beaters. Do not over beat. Spoon onto a baking sheet covered with parchment paper or use a pastry bag for fancier shapes. For a glaze you may sprinkle lightly with granulated sugar. Bake for one hour, turn the oven off, open the door, and do not disturb for at least five minutes. When cool, place meringues immediately in an air tight container. Do not freeze.

SOFT and SPICY GINGER COOKIES

These are a welcome change to the usual store bought ginger snaps. With plenty of zippy sweetness, they are the perfect accompaniment to afternoon tea. Children (and many adults) love these with a glass of ice cold milk. To make skim milk more palatable add one or two ice cubes. The colder the milk, the better it tastes. Be warned, however, that though you may plan to freeze these cookies, they will probably be gobbled up and never make it to the freezer!

Preheat oven to 350°

Ingredients

1 ¼ cups presifted flour

2 teaspoons ground cinnamon

1 teaspoon ground cloves

½ teaspoon nutmeg

½ teaspoon powdered ginger

1 teaspoon baking soda

¼ teaspoon sea salt

1 cup brown sugar, packed lightly

¼ cup canola oil

⅓ cup molasses

1 extra large egg, room temperature

1 ¼ cups chopped crystallized ginger

Granulated sugar

Procedure

Line 2 cookie sheets with parchment paper. Sift together the flour, cinnamon, cloves, nutmeg, ginger, baking soda, and sea salt. Set aside.

cont...

In a separate bowl, use an electric mixer on medium speed and beat the brown sugar, canola oil, and molasses for about 3 minutes. Reduce speed to low, add the egg, and beat for an additional 1 minute. Keeping the mixer on low, very slowly and gradually add the dry ingredients until well combined. Now stir in the crystallized ginger.

Scoop out the dough for each cookie with a spoon, then use your fingers to form into a ball about 2 inches in diameter. Flatten slightly.

Add granulated sugar to a shallow flat bottomed dish and press both sides of the cookies into the sugar to coat. Place on the cookie sheets and bake for no more than 13 minutes. The cookies should be soft in the center and will appear slightly crackled on the surface. Allow the cookies to cool on the pans for 2 minutes, then transfer to a cooling rack. Pack completely cooled cookies in an air tight container if you wish to freeze.

Makes 16 large cookies.

"We are indeed much more than what we eat, but what we eat can nevertheless help us to be much more than what we are."

—Adelle Davis

Sauces

&

Such

BASTING SAUCE FOR CHICKEN

Ingredients

8 ounces tomato sauce (homemade or store bought)

5 tablespoons molasses

¼ cup apple cider vinegar

2 tablespoons Worcestershire sauce

1 tablespoon soy sauce

1 tablespoon Dijon mustard

1 teaspoon dried thyme or 1 tablespoon chopped fresh

⅛ teaspoon freshly ground black pepper

Procedure

Combine all ingredients in a saucepan. Bring to a boil while stirring, then simmer until reduced to a thick sauce (about 30 minutes).

Makes one cup or enough for basting one whole chicken.

"The most remarkable thing about my mother is that for thirty years she served the family leftovers. The original has never been found."

—Calvin Trillin

Jeannie Serpa

FRESH TOMATO SAUCE

Store bought tomato sauces are often high in saturated fat and extremely high in sodium and sugar. This fresh sauce is quick and easy to prepare and has none of the negative qualities of tomato sauce in a can or jar.

Ingredients

¼ cup extra virgin olive oil

½ cup chopped green pepper

¼ cup chopped onion

2 cloves garlic, minced

1 teaspoon oregano

2 teaspoons marjoram

1 teaspoon thyme

⅓ cup chopped parsley

¼ cup chopped fresh basil, loosely packed or 1 teaspoon dried

6 cups cubed fresh tomatoes (about 6 or 7)

Sea salt and fresh ground pepper to taste

Procedure

Heat olive oil in a heavy saucepan. Add green pepper and onion. Cook until tender soft, then add garlic and herbs. Continue cooking for 2 minutes, then add tomatoes. Season with salt and pepper. Simmer an additional 15 minutes. Serve over pasta or rice.

Makes 3 cups.

GINGER BARBEQUE SAUCE

Use this lively, aromatic combination as a marinade for vegetables, or warm it over low heat and serve as a sauce.

Ingredients

½ cup soy sauce

½ cup ketchup

¼ cup dry white wine

3 tablespoons brown sugar

2 tablespoons grated fresh ginger

Procedure

Whisk all ingredients together until well combined. Add vegetables and toss gently. Allow to marinate for 10 to 20 minutes and grill over medium heat until tender crisp.

"Preach not to others what they should eat, but eat as becomes you and be silent."

—Epictetus

GREAT GRANOLA

This is a super-delicious, easy way to make granola. The oats, almonds, and pecans place it high on my list of cholesterol fighters. Store in an air tight container. The apricots and cranberries add not only antioxidants, but soluble fiber as well.

Preheat oven to 300°

Ingredients

6 cups old fashion oatmeal (rolled oats)
¼ cup chopped pecans
¼ cup chopped almonds
2 tablespoons brown sugar
½ teaspoon salt
¼ cup honey
1 ⅓ cups pure maple syrup
¼ cup pineapple juice
1 teaspoon almond extract
Canola baking spray
¼ cup chopped dried apricots
¼ cup dried cranberries

Procedure

In a large bowl, combine oatmeal, pecans, almonds, sugar, and salt. Add honey, maple syrup, pineapple juice, and almond extract. Mix thoroughly. Coat a jelly roll pan or cookie sheet with the canola spray. Spread mixture evenly in the pan and bake for 45 minutes, being sure to stir every 15 minutes. Remove from oven and mix in the apricots and cranberries. Cool completely.

Yield: 10 half cup servings.

MAKE BELIEVE MAYO

I'm not about to claim that this tastes like the real thing; however, this is a tasty spread that you'll love on sandwiches, salads, and as a dip with raw vegetables. Regular mayonnaise contains about 1.5 grams of saturated (bad) fat per serving of 2 tablespoons. This has none whatever. Give it a try !

Ingredients

1 (6 ounce) container fat free plain yogurt

2 tablespoons fat free lemon yogurt

Paprika

Black pepper

Procedure

Combine the two yogurts. Add a pinch of paprika and a dash or two of black pepper. This will keep in your refrigerator for as long as the expiration date on the yogurt containers.

Makes ¾ of a cup.

MOCK HOLLANDAISE

A traditional Hollandaise Sauce recipe contains a ½ cup of butter and 3 egg yolks, both no-no's for us cholesterol watchers. Here is a better alternative that is not only delicious, but simple to make. I actually prefer its flavor to the real thing. Mock Hollandaise has the added advantage of being a do ahead sauce that can be refrigerated and reheated. Enjoy!

cont...

Ingredients

1 cup reduced fat mayonnaise

3 extra large egg whites

3 tablespoons fresh lemon juice

½ teaspoon dry mustard

½ teaspoon sea salt

⅛ teaspoon fresh ground black pepper

1 tablespoon chopped fresh dill or 1 teaspoon dried

¼ cup skimmed milk or fat free half & half cream

Procedure

In a saucepan, whisk together all ingredients, except milk, stirring constantly over medium heat until smooth. This makes a thick sauce. Now stir in milk, adding more if needed. Warm to desired temperature. Delicious served over steamed asparagus, green beans, or any white fish.

Makes about 1 ½ cups.

PUMPKIN APPLE BUTTER

Serve this zero fat, zero cholesterol sweet butter as a topping for hot oatmeal or oat bran cereal. Use also as a delicious spread on oat bran muffins or toast. An added benefit is the pumpkin, which contains significant amounts of beta-carotene. Beta-carotene is a key nutrient that aides our bodies in manufacturing vitamin A.

Ingredients

1 can (15 ounce) pumpkin

1 medium apple, peeled and grated

cont...

1 cup apple juice

½ cup packed brown sugar

¾ teaspoon pumpkin pie spice

Procedure

Combine pumpkin, apple, apple juice, sugar, and pumpkin pie spice in medium, heavy-duty saucepan. Bring to boil; reduce heat to low. Cook, stirring occasionally, 1 ½ hours.

Store in airtight container in refrigerator up to 2 months.

RASPBERRY - CRANBERRY SAUCE

Excellent accompaniment for chicken and turkey.

Ingredients

10 ounce package unsweetened frozen raspberries, thawed

1 cup water

1 pound fresh cranberries, washed and drained

1 ½ cups sugar

Procedure

Strain raspberries, reserve juice and set aside.

In a large saucepan, combine water, reserved juice, cranberries, and sugar.

Bring to a boil and cook until the cranberries pop open. Stir in raspberries and chill.

RASPBERRY SAUCE

Use this fruit sauce over non fat frozen yogurt or pour over slices of Angel Food Cake.

Ingredients

1 (10 ounce) jar seedless raspberry jam

3 tablespoons orange juice

2 tablespoons lime juice

Procedure

Combine jam, orange juice, and lime juice in a saucepan. Warm over medium heat, stirring constantly. Serve warm or at room temperature. Cooled sauce can be refrigerated and used cold or reheated.

Children's
Recipes

EMILIE'S APPLES n' DIP

This yummy little snack is high in antioxidants and though peanuts contain fat, they have been proven to reduce blood cholesterol. Start teaching small children while they are young, explaining that our bodies need some fat and some cholesterol, but that there are good fats and bad fats. Keep it simple and above all, keep it fun!

Ingredients

2 large apples, peeled and cored

3 tablespoons peanut butter

6 ounce container fat free plain yogurt

Procedure

An adult should peel, core, and slice the apples. Meanwhile, the kids can be measuring and mixing peanut butter and yogurt in a small bowl. When ready, they'll simply dip apple slices in the peanut butter mix and indulge.

Serves 4.

HANNAH BANANA SUNDAE

The key ingredient to a Hannah Banana Sundae is IMAGINATION. This recipe was developed by my granddaughter, Hannah Burke Serpa.

Ingredients

Sliced bananas

Non fat frozen vanilla yogurt (resembles real ice cream, but better for you)

Fruit of choice (chopped cherries, peaches, strawberries, blueberries, kiwis)

One or more of these for crunch: low fat granola, sliced almonds, chopped walnuts, or crushed whole grain cereal

Your favorite topping (any flavor non fat yogurt, low fat caramel or chocolate sauce, honey or low fat whipped cream)

Procedure

Place a scoop of non fat frozen yogurt in a serving bowl. Cover with sliced bananas, then add your favorite fruit. Drizzle with whatever topping you choose and finish off with a sprinkle of crunch. Use your imagination. You may think of other ingredients, so go for it!

Hannah Burke Serpa

KIDS' STUFFED CELERY

You don't have to be a child to love these. I serve them to grownups as an appetizer and kids love making them for a healthy afternoon snack. Small children can manage this simple recipe, which is safe for them with no cooking involved.

Ingredients

12 celery sticks, peeled, with strings removed

½ cup peanut butter

½ cup Yogurt Cheese *

2 tablespoons granola or Cheerios, slightly crushed

Procedure

Kids can make the Yogurt Cheese ahead of time. It will keep in the refrigerator for as long as the expiration date printed on the container. An adult can be stringing and cutting celery stalks into sticks while the children prepare the stuffing. Have them mix the peanut butter, yogurt cheese and granola together, then fill each celery stick.

Serves 4 or 5.

*YOGURT CHEESE

12 ounces plain, fat free yogurt (2 six ounce containers). Line a wire strainer with a coffee filter and place over a bowl. Spoon in the yogurt and let drain for two hours in the refrigerator. Discard the liquid.

KIDS' STYLE HUMMUS

Most small children (and many adults too) find hummus a bit too strong for their tastes. Here is a way to tone down Lemon Hummus and sweeten it too. Children can mix this themselves and learn a bit about measuring ingredients at the same time. Since hummus is made from garbanzo beans, which are high on my list of FIGHTER FOODS, this recipe is especially healthy and cholesterol friendly.

Ingredients

- 1 (6 ounce) container fat free lemon hummus
- 1 (6 ounce) container fat free plain yogurt
- 3 tablespoons fat free or lite lemon yogurt (increase amount according to taste)

Procedure

Mix all ingredients in a small bowl. Makes over 12 ounces. Serve with baked potato chips or rice crackers (KA-ME is an excellent brand that kids love.)

"Water is the most neglected nutrient in your diet but one of the most vital."

—Kelly Barton

LITTLE GREEN TREES in the FOREST

Broccoli may not be a favorite with most children, but this rendition could change their minds. Warning: adults love these too. Don't be surprised when one of these "forests" shows up at a cocktail party!

Ingredients

¼ cup olive oil

1 tablespoon vinegar

1 tablespoon granulated sugar (or more to taste)

16 ounce package frozen broccoli florets

Sea salt

1 loaf of unsliced bread

Procedure

Children can remove florets from the freezer, open the package and place them in a large bowl to thaw. Help them to measure the oil, vinegar, and sugar and combine in a small bowl. Pour the mixture over the broccoli. Stir gently, sprinkle lightly with salt, and place in refrigerator to marinate for at least one hour.

Remove from refrigerator. Spear florets with toothpicks and "plant" each tree in the top of the bread loaf, covering it and creating a "forest."

MONKEY SANDWICHES

Bananas are rich in vitamin K, potassium, and antioxidants. Peanuts are not nuts; they are legumes. But like nuts, they have been proven to lower cholesterol.

Ingredients

1 small can lightly salted peanuts

4 small or two large bananas

8 slices bread

Procedure

Place peanuts in a 12 inch zip lock bag. Squeeze out air and seal bag completely. Crush peanuts with a wooden mallet or bottom of a small pan. Such fun!

To prevent banana "strings," turn bananas upside down to peel. Place bananas on a large plate and mash with a folk. For each child, spread a layer of mashed bananas on two slices of bread. Sprinkle crushed peanuts on one slice of bread. Place second slice on top and devour!

Enough for 4 sandwiches.

QUINN'S FAVORITE SNACK

We need to be aware of cholesterol problems in our children before they start, particularly in families with a history of heart disease. This is simple enough for even 4 and 5 year olds to prepare. It's also a fun math lesson. Have them count out the crackers, figure out how many grape halves are needed, or count out 3 raisins to a cracker.

Ingredients

12 rice crackers (KA-ME is an excellent brand)

Peanut butter, smooth or crunchy

6 grapes, halved (substitute 24 whole raisins)

Procedure

An adult can be cutting the grapes in half while the children spread peanut butter on the crackers. They can then top with grapes or use 3 raisins to a cracker.

Serves 2-4, depending on appetites.

"If more of us valued food and cheer and song above hoarded gold, it would be a merrier world."

—J.R.R. Tolkien

SAND DUNES

This is a fun recipe for children aged 4 to 8. The best part for them is smashing the Cheerios! It's an excellent lesson in math too, since they get to measure the ingredients themselves. Cheerios provide soluble fiber, a well known cholesterol fighter, and the fat free cheese is full of protein and has no saturated fat.

Ingredients

1 cup Cheerios

2 cups fat free cream cheese or fat free frozen yogurt, flavor of choice (Kemp's is an excellent brand)

2 tablespoons honey or maple syrup

1 tablespoon raisins

Procedure

Put Cheerios in a zip lock bag, push out air and seal. Smash with a wooden mallet or bottom of a small pot until the Cheerios are pulverized.

For each serving, place half a cup of cream cheese in a shallow bowl and shape into a mound. Drizzle with honey or maple syrup. Lightly sprinkle "sand" (crushed Cheerios) over the mound, covering the honey completely. Scatter a few raisins (rocks) around the base.

SPECIAL FUN APPLESAUCE

Adults will need to read this recipe to small children and allow them to carry out the instructions. This may look like dessert and taste like dessert, but it is nutritious enough to be eaten for breakfast.

Ingredients

1 (6 ounce) container fat free plain yogurt

6 ounces applesauce

½ teaspoon cinnamon

1 teaspoon brown sugar

½ cup Cheerios

Procedure

Empty the container of yogurt into a large cereal bowl. Fill the empty yogurt container with applesauce. This is an easy way to measure the 6 ounces of applesauce. Now add the applesauce to the bowl of yogurt and stir together. Use measuring spoons to measure the cinnamon and brown sugar. Add both to the mixture. Divide this mixture into 2 dessert bowls. Sprinkle each with one half of the Cheerios.

"There is no sincerer love than the love of food."

—George Bernard Shaw

TINY TARTS FOR TINY TOTS

These are easy for little ones to assemble. Start your children early with cholesterol friendly foods that they can prepare themselves.

Ingredients

Store bought frozen mini tarts (Athen's has no saturated fat)
Peanut butter
Grape or other flavored jelly or jam

Procedure

Defrost tarts. Fill each tart with ¾ teaspoon peanut butter, top with one teaspoon jelly, and gobble these up!

> *"If the divine creator has taken pains to give us delicious and exquisite things to eat, the least we can do is prepare them well and serve them with ceremony."*
>
> —Fernand Point

YOGURT PEANUT BUTTER FUN

Children love to take part in food preparation and are more likely to eat what they prepare. Here is a no-cook snack that kids can fix themselves. Peanuts are a legume, not a nut as their name implies. They are on the list of foods that have been proven to help reduce cholesterol and all children seem to love peanut butter.

Ingredients

6 ounce container fat free plain yogurt

2 tablespoons peanut butter (smooth or chunky) at room temperature

1 or 2 teaspoons raisins

Procedure

Combine peanut butter and yogurt, adding more peanut butter to taste. This takes a bit of stirring, so encourage your child to keep at it. This is a fun project and gives kids a chance to taste test and add as much peanut butter as they like.

Add the raisins and enjoy!

Serves 1.

About the Author

Jeannie Serpa, mother of nine and grandmother of eighteen (so far), brings to this book an abundance of experience and knowledge. A former school teacher, stencil designer, business entrepreneur, and writer of restaurant reviews, Jeannie has embarked on a four year journey researching and developing recipes designed to lower cholesterol. This undertaking has a very personal connection since many of her family members have been victims of heart attacks, strokes, and other cholesterol health related diseases.

In January of 2004, Jeannie was told her cholesterol level was dangerously high, and a statin drug was prescribed. Nine days on the drug resulted in extreme muscular pain and stiffness. She flushed those tablets down the toilet, embarked on a research program, and started developing recipes, using ingredients that had been proven to reduce cholesterol. Six weeks later she returned to her doctor with a vastly improved cholesterol count. When she announced that she hadn't taken the prescribed drug in six weeks, the physician was stunned.

Jeannie has authored six books in the field of decorative arts and has written for numerous craft and home décor publications. She has done several videos and appeared on national TV shows including PBS' *This Old House* with Bob Villa. She currently writes food related articles for *South County Living Magazine* and a monthly column called <u>Effortless Entertaining</u> for two newspapers: *The Northeast Independent* and *The South County Independent*.

In the works are two more books: <u>Eating Your Way To Low Cholesterol, Volume #2</u> and a mystery thriller that features a character who just happens to be a cookbook author! Ms. Serpa lives, cooks and writes in Rhode Island and New Hampshire.

INDEX

Poultry

Apricot Sweet and Sour Chicken 172

Chicken a l'Orange # 1 174

Chicken a l'Orange # 2 175

Chicken Farmer's Pie 177

Crispy Baked Chicken with Garlicky Spinach 179

Grilled Rosemary Chicken 180

Honey Lime Chicken Breast 182

Lemon Chicken Salad 183

Mini Meatballs with Angel Hair Pasta 184

Oven Fried Chicken with Raspberry Sauce 186

Rackless Roasted Chicken 188

Skillet Chicken Breasts with Apricot Gravy 190

Turkey Meat Loaf 192

Seafood

Cajun Shrimp over Jasmine Rice 194

Calamari Salad with Mushrooms and Avocados 195

Crab Salad Finger Rolls 197

Crab Salad with Lemon Caper Dressing 198

Deep Fried Calamari in a Beer Batter 199

Gourmet Tuna Rolls 201

Lemon Pepper Swordfish, Baked or Grilled 202

Lobster Linguine 203

Lobsterman's Pie 205

Monkfish with Basil Mayonnaise 206

Mussels Steamed in Wine 208

Open Salmon Salad Sandwich 209

Roasted Citrus Salmon 209

Salmon Cakes 211

Scrod with Wine Rosemary Demi Glaze 212

Speedy Microwave Salmon, # 1 214

Speedy Microwave Salmon, # 2 215

Swordfish in Sour Cream Mushroom Sauce 216

Tomato Dressed Cod over Pasta 217

Tropical Lobster Salad 218

Zesty Baked Flounder 220

Muffins

Apple Raisin Oat Bran 85

Autumn Oat Bran 86

Banana Nut 88

Blueberry 89

Carrot Cake 91

Cranberry Mandarin Orange 92

Lemon Blueberry Oat Bran 94

Pineapple Pecan 95

Pumpkin Pie 96

Pumpkin, Pineapple, Pecan 98

Raspberry Surprise 99

Triple A Super 101

Salads

Broccoli Cashew Salad 105

Broccoli Slaw 15

Calamari Salad with Mushrooms and Avocados 195

Crab Salad Finger Rolls 197

Crabmeat Salad with Lemon Caper Dressing 198

Christmas Pear Salad 107

Citrus Winter Salad 107

Colorful Cabbage Slaw 109

Fancy Fruit Salad 110

Fruit Salad with Raspberry Yogurt Dressing 111

Breinigsville, PA USA
01 December 2009
228389BV00002B/2/P